GOOD HOME
BAKING

GOOD HOME BAKING

Mary Cadogan

CONTENTS

First published in 1983 by Octopus Books Limited
59 Grosvenor Street, London W1

Second impression, 1984

© 1983 Hennerwood Publications Limited

ISBN 0 86273 067 8

Produced by Mandarin Publishers Limited
22a Westlands Road
Quarry Bay
Hong Kong

Printed in Hong Kong

INTRODUCTION

The secret to becoming a good cook is to start with the basics. There are surprisingly few skills to master before you can produce a wealth of cakes, biscuits and bakes. Of course the glorious confections that take days of concentration to produce will be daunting, however, the recipes here are chosen to help you achieve perfect results every time, with quick methods and a little cheating where appropriate. Icings and decorations are mainly simple, with a few elaborate cakes to inspire you.

Each chapter concentrates on one or two techniques starting with the simplest ideas and going on to more elaborate ones.

Creaming
This method in which fat and sugar are beaten to a light creamy texture forms the basis of many rich flavoursome cakes and bakes. Butter is the first choice for creamed cakes, as it gives the best flavour. However, as it is a hard fat, it can be arm-aching work, so the softer good quality margarines make an easier substitute. Caster sugar gives the finished cake a fine texture, although for rich cakes a soft brown sugar is more often used. For ease of working, bring the butter to room temperature before using it. When using a mixer, heat it up by filling the bowl with hot water, put in the blades and leave for a few minutes. Pour out the water and dry the bowl and blades. Creaming will be much easier with warm utensils.

Rubbing in, Rolling and Folding
This chapter gives detailed instructions for making pastries ranging from the traditional shortcrust (with many variations) to a simple rough puff pastry and on to the more involved flaky pastries. To achieve light results, try to handle the pastry as little as possible. When kneading it, treat it firmly and your dough will soon become smooth. When rolling and folding the pastry to make puff pastries, try to keep the corners as squared up as possible to give plenty of airy layers and chill it well between stages.

Melting and Whisking
Melt fat and sugar, tip in the remaining ingredients and you have the key to a variety of delicious sticky and substantial cakes, from gingerbread and parkin to florentines and passion cake. Melted cakes tend to have rich spicy flavourings so the fat you use is not so crucial as it is for creamed cakes. Lard, margarine and butter all have their uses in melted recipes. An extra raising agent in the form of baking powder or bicarbonate of soda gives the cakes a lighter texture.

Whisking eggs and sugar to a light foam for fluffy cakes and gâteaux requires a little more concentration but the results are certainly worth it. Take the phone off the hook to make sure you aren't disturbed. You will notice when whisking the eggs and sugar that the mixture starts off yellow and fairly liquid. It will gradually change as you whisk to a pale, thick creamy foam. It is not until you can leave a trail in the mixture when you lift the beaters, that the mixture is ready for the flour. Keep eggs for whisking at room temperature, they will then whisk to the greatest volume for a lighter cake. Sift the flour all together on to the surface of the foam and use a large metal spoon to fold it in. The technique is to cut through the mixture and turn it over to incorporate the flour without knocking out the air. This step is always easier if the eggs and sugar have been sufficiently whisked.

Yeasted Bakes

Traditional breads and cakes are included here. Dried yeast has been used for the recipes as it is most commonly available. For fresh yeast, use 15 g (½ oz) in place of 1–2 teaspoons dried yeast, or 25 g (1 oz) fresh instead of 1 tablespoon (15 g/½ oz) dried. Blend the fresh yeast with warm liquid, omitting the sugar and it is ready to use straight away. Dried yeast is left to froth for a short time to give it a good start before adding it to the flour. Some new types of dried yeast can be added directly to the flour, in which case follow the instructions on the pack.

All-in-one

Simple one-step methods using soft margarines and oils bypass the normal rules to produce quick, foolproof results. Choux pastry is included here as the technique is so simple – the secret is in careful weighing of the ingredients to give a dough of the right consistency. Have the flour for your choux pastry weighed out and sifted on to a plate before you start. It can then be tipped quickly into the boiling fat and water. Beat the mixture well, when adding the flour, to give a smooth batter. When the mixture forms a thick ball and comes away from the sides of the saucepan you can stop beating and cool it for a minute or so before adding the beaten eggs. Choux pastry rises and crisps at a fairly high temperature. For larger choux puffs it is necessary to then decrease the oven temperature to cook the pastry completely without burning it.

Various cooking 'cheats' are used in this chapter. These include cakes made with soft margarine and a little extra baking powder instead of creaming the cake; using melted butter or vegetable oil; using soft margarine to make a quick rich pastry, and even making a Christmas cake 'all-in-one'.

Freezing instructions are not given with the recipes as, generally speaking, they all freeze beautifully. Wrap cakes in foil or freezer film. More decorative ones should first be open frozen before wrapping or storing in a rigid container. Pack biscuits into boxes or freezer bags. The dough for Ginger whirls (page 75) and Nut choc chip biscuits (page 37) can be frozen unbaked and sliced off as needed. Most cakes will store for up to 6 months.

The equipment necessary for baking is fairly minimal. If you have a mixing bowl, wooden spoon, scales and rolling pin, you can make most of the cakes in this book. An electric whisk or mixer will help enormously with the laborious jobs like creaming and whisking. A food processor is excellent for rubbing fat into flour in seconds and competent for creaming mixtures. As the food processor works at such a high speed, beware of overworking the ingredients for pastry and shortbreads. I find it is best to work the ingredients in short blasts, to enable me to check progress.

Just a few baking tins will serve you for most of your baking. Useful tins include a 20 cm (8 inch) deep round cake tin; 18–20 cm (7–8 inch) sandwich tins; a 23 cm × 33 cm (9 inch × 13 inch) Swiss roll tin which can double as a baking sheet; a 28 cm × 18 cm (7 inch × 11 inch) shallow oblong tin for tray bakes and biscuits and a 1 kg (2 lb) loaf tin. Non-stick tins are a useful plus except when you are making pastry, when the tins do not need greasing, non-stick or otherwise. Non-stick silicone paper is excellent for lining tins and can be wiped clean for using again.

Give non-stick tins a light greasing before use, although there is no need to line them with greaseproof paper. In general when lining tins, the quicker cooking cakes need just bottom lining and the richer cakes such as fruit cakes, which have a long cooking time, need the base and sides of the tin lined, to help protect the cakes from burning.

M This symbol used against some of the titles denotes a master recipe. These are basic recipes for processes such as making shortcrust pastry or white bread. The recipes give detailed step-by-step instructions for the particular process. If making up subsequent recipes using a master technique, it is worth reading through the master for full information.

CREAMING

MARBLED BARS

Makes 24 bars
175 g (6 oz) butter or margarine
175 g (6 oz) caster sugar
3 eggs, beaten
175 g (6 oz) self-raising flour
few drops of red food colouring
1 tablespoon cocoa
2 tablespoons boiling water
Fudge icing:
50 g (2 oz) plain chocolate, broken up
50 g (2 oz) butter
225 g (8 oz) icing sugar, sifted
2 tablespoons milk

Preparation time: 30 minutes
Cooking time: 25–30 minutes
Oven: 180°C, 350°F, Gas Mark 4

1. Grease an 18 cm × 28 cm (7 inch × 11 inch) shallow oblong tin.
2. Place the butter or margarine and sugar in a bowl. Beat with a wooden spoon for 10 minutes, or in a mixer for 5 minutes, until light and fluffy.
3. Beat in the eggs, a little at a time.
4. Add the flour to the mixture, folding in lightly using a metal spoon.
5. Divide the mixture in half. Colour one half pink with a few drops of red food colouring. Blend the cocoa with the water to a smooth paste and mix into the other half of the mixture.
6. Place alternate spoonsful of each flavour side by side in the prepared tin. Swirl the two mixtures together with a skewer, then level off the top with a spoon.
7. Bake in a preheated oven for 25–30 minutes, until risen and golden. Leave in the tin to cool.
8. Place all the fudge icing ingredients into a bowl over a saucepan of hot water. Stir until smooth and glossy, then remove from the heat, and leave until thick enough for spreading.
9. Spread the icing evenly over the top of the cake, swirling it with a round-ended knife.
10. Cut the cake into 3 down the length and 8 across to make 24 bars.

FROSTED COFFEE CAKE M

Makes one 20 cm (8 inch) cake
175 g (6 oz) butter or margarine
175 g (6 oz) caster sugar
3 eggs, beaten
175 g (6 oz) self-raising flour
2 tablespoons strong black coffee
Icing:
225 g (8 oz) icing sugar, sifted
50 g (2 oz) butter
2 tablespoons strong black coffee

Preparation time: 20 minutes
Cooking time: 30 minutes
Oven: 180°C, 350°F, Gas Mark 4

1. Grease and bottom line two 20 cm (8 inch) round sandwich tins.
2. To make the cake, place the butter and sugar in a bowl. Mix together with a wooden spoon, then beat for 10 minutes until the mixture is light and fluffy, scraping down the sides of the bowl at intervals. Alternatively, beat in a mixer for 5 minutes.
3. Add the beaten eggs a little at a time, beating well between each addition.
4. Add the flour and fold in lightly with a metal tablespoon, cutting through the mixture and turning it over until the flour is evenly mixed. Lightly fold in the coffee.
5. Divide the mixture between the 2 prepared tins. Level the tops with the back of a metal spoon.
6. Bake in a preheated oven for 30 minutes until the cakes are golden brown and spring back when pressed with the fingers.
7. Turn out the cakes, remove the paper and cool on a wire tray.
8. To make the icing, place the icing ingredients in a bowl over a saucepan of hot water. Heat gently, stirring until smooth and glossy. Remove the pan from the heat.
9. Leave the icing until it is cold, then beat until thick enough to spread.
10. Place 1 sandwich cake on a serving plate. Spread with half the icing. Cover with the other cake. Spread the top with the remaining icing, swirling with a round-ended knife.

Frosted coffee cake; Marbled bars

ST CLEMENT'S CAKE

Makes one 20 cm (8 inch) cake
175 g (6 oz) butter or margarine
175 g (6 oz) caster sugar
3 eggs, beaten
grated rind of 1 lemon
175 g (6 oz) self-raising flour
Icing:
225 g (8 oz) icing sugar, sifted
75 g (3 oz) butter
1 teaspoon grated orange rind
2 tablespoons orange juice
few drops of orange food colouring
orange and lemon jelly slices, to decorate

Preparation time: 25 minutes
Cooking time: 30 minutes
Oven: 180°C, 350°F, Gas Mark 4

1. Grease and bottom-line two 20 cm (8 inch) sandwich tins.
2. Place the butter or margarine and sugar in a bowl. Beat with a wooden spoon for 10 minutes, or in a mixer for 5 minutes, until light and fluffy.
3. Beat in the eggs, a little at a time.
4. Stir in the lemon rind. Add the flour and fold in lightly with a metal spoon until evenly mixed.
5. Divide the mixture between the 2 prepared tins. Smooth the top of each with the back of a spoon.
6. Bake in a preheated oven for 30 minutes until the cakes are golden brown and spring back when pressed with the fingers. Turn out and leave to cool on a wire tray.
7. Place all the icing ingredients in a bowl. Mix, then beat for 2 minutes until light and creamy.
8. Sandwich the 2 cakes together with one-third of the icing. Spread the remaining icing over the top and sides of the cake. Mark with a fork in wavy lines.
9. Decorate with orange and lemon jelly slices.

SULTANA CAKE

Makes one 18 cm (7 inch) cake
150 g (5 oz) butter or margarine
150 g (5 oz) soft dark brown sugar
2 eggs, beaten
350 g (12 oz) sultanas
120 ml (4 fl oz) milk
100 g (4 oz) self-raising flour
100 g (4 oz) wheatmeal flour
1 teaspoon mixed spice

Preparation time: 20 minutes
Cooking time: 1¾–2 hours
Oven: 160°C, 325°F, Gas Mark 3

1. Grease and bottom line an 18 cm (7 inch) round cake tin.
2. Place the butter or margarine and sugar in a bowl. Beat with a wooden spoon for 10 minutes, or in a mixer for 5 minutes, until light and fluffy.
3. Beat in the eggs, a little at a time.
4. Stir in the sultanas and milk. Add the flours and the spice and fold in lightly using a metal spoon.
5. Place the mixture in a greased and bottom-lined 18 cm (7 inch) round cake tin.
6. Bake in a preheated oven for 1¾–2 hours until the cake is golden brown and springs back when pressed with the fingers.
7. Cool in the tin for 15 minutes, then turn out and cool on a wire tray.

VANILLA RING CAKE

Makes one 20 cm (8 inch) ring
100 g (4 oz) butter
50 g (2 oz) honey
50 g (2 oz) caster sugar
2 eggs, beaten
1 teaspoon vanilla essence
100 g (4 oz) self-raising flour
Icing and decoration:
100 g (4 oz) icing sugar, sifted
2 tablespoons hot water
few drops of vanilla essence
2 teaspoons chopped nuts, toasted

Preparation time: 20 minutes
Cooking time: 35 minutes
Oven: 180°C, 350°F, Gas Mark 4

St Clement's cake; Vanilla ring cake

MADEIRA CAKE

Makes one 15 cm (6 inch) cake
175 g (6 oz) butter
175 g (6 oz) caster sugar
3 eggs, beaten
225 g (8 oz) plain flour
1 teaspoon baking powder
grated rind of ½ lemon
strip of citron peel (optional)

Preparation time: 20 minutes
Cooking time: 1½ hours
Oven: 160°C, 325°F, Gas Mark 3

1. Grease and bottom line a 15 cm (6 inch) round cake tin.
2. Place the butter and sugar in a bowl. Beat with a wooden spoon for 10 minutes, or in a mixer for 5 minutes, until light and fluffy.
3. Beat in the eggs, a little at a time.
4. Sift the flour and baking powder into the bowl. Fold them into the mixture using a metal spoon. Fold in the lemon rind.
5. Place the mixture in the prepared tin. Smooth the top. If using, place the strip of citron peel in the centre of the cake.
6. Bake in a preheated oven for 1½ hours until the cake has risen and is light golden in colour. When cooked the cake should spring back when pressed with the fingers.
7. Turn out and cool on a wire tray.

1. Grease and flour a 20 cm (8 inch) ring mould.
2. Place the butter, honey and sugar in a bowl. Beat with a wooden spoon for 10 minutes, or in a mixer for 5 minutes, until light and fluffy.
3. Beat in the eggs, a little at a time.
4. Stir in the vanilla essence. Add the flour and fold into the mixture lightly with a metal spoon.
5. Turn into the prepared ring mould. Bake in a preheated oven for 35 minutes until the cake is golden brown and springs back when pressed with the fingers.
6. Turn out and cool on a wire tray.
7. Beat the water into the icing sugar until the mixture coats the back of a spoon, about 2 minutes. Beat in the vanilla essence.
8. Drizzle the icing over the cake, sprinkle with the chopped nuts and leave to set.

Variation:
Almond and Spice: Omit the vanilla and add 50 g (2 oz) finely chopped blanched almonds and ½ teaspoon mixed spice at step 4.

TOSCA CAKE

Makes one 19 cm (7½ inch) cake
100 g (4 oz) butter
100 g (4 oz) caster sugar
2 eggs, beaten
50 g (2 oz) ground almonds
few drops of almond essence
100 g (4 oz) self-raising flour
Topping:
25 g (1 oz) butter
50 g (2 oz) flaked almonds
50 g (2 oz) caster sugar
1 tablespoon plain flour
1 tablespoon milk

Preparation time: 25 minutes
Cooking time: 45 minutes
Oven: 180°C, 350°F, Gas Mark 4

1. Grease and bottom-line a 19 cm (7½ inch) square shallow tin.
2. Place the 100 g (4 oz) butter and sugar in a bowl. Beat with a wooden spoon for 10 minutes, or in a mixer for 5 minutes, until light and fluffy.
3. Beat in the eggs, a little at a time.
4. Add the ground almonds, almond essence and flour, then fold in lightly using a metal spoon.
5. Turn the mixture into the prepared tin and smooth the top with the back of a spoon.
6. Place on a baking sheet and bake in a preheated oven for 30 minutes until just cooked. After 25 minutes make the topping.
7. Melt the butter in a saucepan. Add the remaining topping ingredients and heat gently, stirring constantly, until the sugar has melted.
8. After the cake has been cooking for 30 minutes, remove from the oven and spread the topping over it. Return to the oven for a further 15 minutes.
9. Cool in the tin, then cut into 12 squares.

ORANGE JAPONAISE GÂTEAU

Serves 8
50 g (2 oz) butter
50 g (2 oz) caster sugar
1 egg, beaten
grated rind of ½ orange
50 g (2 oz) self-raising flour
2 tablespoons orange juice
3 tablespoons sherry

Japonaise:
2 egg whites
100 g (4 oz) caster sugar
75 g (3 oz) ground almonds

To finish:
25 g (1 oz) plain chocolate
300 ml (½ pint) double cream
1 × 425 g (15 oz) can mandarin oranges, drained

Preparation time: 35 minutes
Cooking time: 1 hour 10 minutes
Oven: 180°C, 350°F, Gas Mark 4;
     150°C, 300°F, Gas Mark 2

1. Grease and bottom-line a 20 cm (8 inch) sandwich cake tin.
2. Place the butter and sugar in a bowl. Beat with a wooden spoon for 10 minutes, or a mixer for 5 minutes, until light and fluffy.
3. Beat in the eggs, a little at a time.
4. Stir in the orange rind. Add the flour and fold in lightly using a metal spoon.
5. Turn the mixture into the prepared tin. Smooth over the top and bake in a preheated oven for 30 minutes, until the cake is golden brown and springs back when pressed with the fingers.
6. Turn out and cool on a wire tray, then sprinkle the orange juice and sherry over the cake.
7. To make the japonaise, reduce the oven temperature. Line a baking sheet with non-stick silicone paper or lightly oiled greaseproof paper and mark it with two 18 cm (7 inch) circles. Lightly grease the paper.
8. Whisk the egg whites in a bowl until stiff. Whisk in half the sugar, then, using a metal spoon, fold in the remainder with the ground almonds, until evenly mixed.
9. Divide the mixture between the circles and spread out evenly up to the marked lines.
10. Bake at the lower temperature for 40 minutes, until firm and lightly browned. Mark 1 circle into 8 wedges.
11. Cool on the baking sheet for 10 minutes, then remove the paper and leave to cool completely on a wire tray. Cut through the marked wedges.
12. Break up the chocolate and place in a small bowl over a saucepan of hot water until it has melted.
13. Place the chocolate in a greaseproof paper bag and snip off a small piece of the corner. Pipe a wavy line of chocolate on each japonaise wedge.
14. Whip the cream until stiff. Place the japonaise circle on a serving plate and spread a layer of a third of the cream over it. Cover with half the oranges.
15. Place the cake on top and spread with another layer of cream. Place the remaining cream in a piping bag fitted with a star tube.
16. Pipe 8 lines on the cake, radiating from the centre. Pipe stars round the edge. Fill the gaps with the remaining oranges. Press the japonaise wedges at an angle into each line of cream. Chill before serving.

Orange japonaise gâteau

DUNDEE CAKE

Makes one 20 cm (8 inch) cake
225 g (8 oz) butter
225 g (8 oz) soft dark brown sugar
5 eggs, beaten
225 g (8 oz) currants
225 g (8 oz) sultanas
225 g (8 oz) raisins
grated rind of 1 orange
grated rind of 1 lemon
50 g (2 oz) glacé cherries, quartered
100 g (4 oz) cut mixed peel
300 g (11 oz) plain flour
2 teaspoons mixed spice
½ teaspoon baking powder
50 g (2 oz) blanched almonds

Preparation time: 25 minutes
Cooking time: 2¾–3 hours
Oven: 160°C, 325°F, Gas Mark 3

1. Grease and line a 20 cm (8 inch) round cake tin.
2. Place the butter and sugar in a large bowl. Beat with a wooden spoon for 10 minutes, or in a mixer for 5 minutes, until light and fluffy.
3. Beat in the eggs, a little at a time.
4. Add the dried fruit, orange and lemon rind, cherries and peel. Mix well.
5. Sift the flour, spice and baking powder into the bowl and fold in using a wooden spoon, until evenly mixed.
6. Turn the mixture into the prepared tin and smooth the top with the back of a spoon. Place the almonds in circles around the top of the cake.
7. Bake in a preheated oven for 2¾–3 hours until the cake is deep golden brown and springs back when pressed with the fingers.
8. Leave to cool in the tin for 30 minutes, then turn out, remove the paper and cool completely on a wire tray. To store, wrap in greaseproof paper, then foil and it will keep for several weeks.

To line the sides, cut greaseproof paper 2 cm (1 inch) longer than the circumference and 5 cm (2 inches) higher than the depth. Fold over the bottom 2 cm (1 inch) and snip.

Cut a circle of greaseproof to fit the bottom of the tin. Fit the side strip inside the tin, so that the snipped edge lies flat. Position the circle over the top.

CRYSTALLIZED FRUIT CAKE

Makes one 18 cm (7 inch) cake
150 g (6 oz) butter
150 g (6 oz) caster sugar
3 eggs, beaten
50 g (2 oz) blanched almonds, chopped
50 g (2 oz) glacé cherries, chopped
25 g (1 oz) crystallized ginger, chopped
25 g (1 oz) crystallized pineapple, chopped
50 g (2 oz) dried apricots, chopped
50 g (2 oz) ground almonds
150 g (6 oz) plain flour
½ teaspoon baking powder
Topping:
2 tablespoons apricot jam
50 g (2 oz) mixed crystallized chopped fruit

Preparation time: 35 minutes
Cooking time: 2½ hours
Oven: 150°C, 300°F, Gas Mark 2

This cake is rich and moist. It makes a delightful alternative to the traditional Christmas cake, which many people find too heavy.

1. Grease and line an 18 cm (7 inch) round cake tin.
2. Place the butter and sugar in a bowl. Beat with a wooden spoon for 10 minutes, or in a mixer for 5 minutes, until light and fluffy.
3. Beat in the eggs, a little at a time.
4. Stir in the chopped almonds, cherries, ginger, pineapple and apricots.
5. Add the ground almonds. Sieve the flour and baking powder into the bowl, then fold into the mixture lightly with a metal spoon until evenly mixed.
6. Place the mixture in the prepared tin and smooth over the top.
7. Bake in a preheated oven for 2½ hours until the cake is light golden and springs back when pressed with the fingers.
8. Leave to cool in the tin for 30 minutes, then turn out, remove the paper and cool on a wire tray.
9. Heat the apricot jam with 1 tablespoon of water, add the chopped crystallized fruit and spread evenly over the top of the cake.

Variation:
To make a light buttery fruit cake, replace the cherries, ginger, pineapple and apricots with 175 g (6 oz) mixed dried fruit or one fruit of your choice. Sprinkle the top of the cake with 50 g (2 oz) chopped nuts before baking it.

CLOCKWISE FROM THE BOTTOM: Dundee cake; Porter cake; Crystallized fruit cake

PORTER CAKE

Makes one 20 cm (8 inch) cake
225 g (8 oz) butter or margarine
225 g (8 oz) soft dark brown sugar
2 eggs, beaten
100 g (4 oz) currants
100 g (4 oz) sultanas
100 g (4 oz) raisins
350 g (12 oz) plain flour
3 teaspoons baking powder
1 teaspoon mixed spice
150 ml (¼ pint) Guinness

Preparation time: 20 minutes
Cooking time: 2¼–2½ hours
Oven: 150°C, 300°F, Gas Mark 2

1. Grease and line a 20 cm (8 inch) round cake tin.
2. Place the butter or margarine and sugar in a bowl. Beat with a wooden spoon for 10 minutes or in a mixer for 5 minutes, until light and fluffy.
3. Beat in the eggs, a little at a time.
4. Stir in the currants, sultanas and raisins.
5. Sift the flour, baking powder and spices into the bowl. Mix lightly until evenly incorporated. Stir in the Guinness.
6. Turn the mixture into the prepared tin. Smooth the top with the back of a metal spoon.
7. Bake in a preheated oven for 2¼–2½ hours until the cake is deep golden brown and springs back when pressed with the fingers.
8. Cool in the tin, then turn out and remove the paper. Wrap in greaseproof paper, then overwrap with foil and store for 2 days before eating.

CHOCOLATE PRALINE FANCIES

Makes 16
100 g (4 oz) butter or margarine
100 g (4 oz) caster sugar
2 eggs, beaten
100 g (4 oz) self-raising flour
Icing and decoration:
175 g (6 oz) caster sugar
75 g (3 oz) hazelnuts
225 g (8 oz) icing sugar, sifted
100 g (4 oz) butter
1 tablespoon cocoa
2 tablespoons boiling water

Preparation time: 30 minutes
Cooking time: 35 minutes
Oven: 160°C, 325°F, Gas Mark 3

1. Grease and bottom-line a 15 cm (6 inch) square cake tin.
2. Place the butter or margarine and sugar in a bowl. Beat with a wooden spoon for 10 minutes or in a mixer for 5 minutes, until light and fluffy.
3. Beat in the eggs, a little at a time.
4. Add the flour and fold in lightly using a metal spoon until evenly mixed.
5. Place the mixture into the prepared tin and smooth over the top.
6. Bake in a preheated oven for 35 minutes, until the cake is golden brown and springs back when pressed with the fingers.
7. Turn out to cool on a wire tray, then cut the cake into 4 each way to make 16 squares.
8. Line a board with foil and grease it.
9. Place the caster sugar and hazelnuts in a heavy-based saucepan. Heat gently until the sugar has dissolved and turns golden brown.
10. Using an oiled teaspoon remove 16 single nuts from the mixture and place them on the foil. Pour the remaining mixture on to the foil away from the single nuts and leave to set.
11. Place the icing sugar and butter in a bowl. Blend the cocoa with boiling water to a paste and add to the bowl. Beat with a wooden spoon until light and creamy.
12. Place the mixture of caramel nuts between 2 sheets of greaseproof paper and crush with a rolling pin, until the praline is broken into small pieces. Transfer to a flat plate or board.
13. Spread a little icing over the sides of the cakes, then roll in the crushed nuts, to coat the sides.
14. Spread a little icing over the top of each cake. Place the remaining icing into a piping bag fitted with a small star tube and pipe stars around the top edges of each cake. Place a single caramel nut in the centre.

CHOCOLATE TOFFEE BARS

Makes 24
175 g (6 oz) butter
75 g (3 oz) caster sugar
250 g (9 oz) plain flour
Topping:
100 g (4 oz) butter
50 g (2 oz) caster sugar
2 tablespoons golden syrup
1 × 200 g (7 oz) can condensed milk
100 g (4 oz) plain or milk chocolate

Preparation time: 25 minutes, plus cooling
Cooking time: 35 minutes
Oven: 160°C, 325°F, Gas Mark 3

1. To make the cake, place the butter and sugar in a bowl. Beat with a wooden spoon for 10 minutes, or in a mixer for 5 minutes, until light and fluffy.
2. Add the flour and mix to a soft dough.
3. Knead the dough lightly on a floured surface, then roll out and line an 18 cm × 28 cm (7 inch × 11 inch) shallow oblong tin.
4. Bake in a preheated oven for 35 minutes, until just beginning to colour. Leave to cool in the tin.
5. To make the topping, place the butter, sugar, syrup and condensed milk in a heavy-based saucepan. Heat gently until the sugar has dissolved, then boil for 5 minutes, stirring until toffee-coloured and thickened.
6. Cool slightly, then spread over the cake. Leave until cold.
7. Break up the chocolate and place in a bowl over a saucepan of hot water until it has melted.
8. Spread the chocolate evenly over the toffee, making wavy lines with a round-ended knife.
9. Leave to set, then cut into 3 lengthways and 8 across.

> If you find the shortbread mixture difficult to roll out, then simply press the dough evenly into the tin using the back of a tablespoon or your fingers.
> When melting the chocolate, check the water under it is not boiling, as this may cause it to curdle.

CLOCKWISE FROM THE BOTTOM: Chocolate toffee bars; Chocolate cup cakes; Chocolate praline fancies

CHOCOLATE CUP CAKES

Makes 24
100 g (4 oz) butter or margarine
100 g (4 oz) caster sugar
2 eggs, beaten
2 tablespoons cocoa
2 tablespoons boiling water
100 g (4 oz) self-raising flour
100 g (4 oz) plain chocolate

Preparation time: 20 minutes
Cooking time: 12–15 minutes
Oven: 190°C, 375°F, Gas Mark 5

1. Place the butter or margarine and sugar in a bowl. Beat with a wooden spoon for 10 minutes or in a mixer for 5 minutes, until light and fluffy.
2. Beat in the eggs, a little at a time.
3. Blend the cocoa and boiling water to a smooth paste, then beat into the cake mixture. Add the flour and fold in lightly with a metal spoon.
4. Line a bun tin with paper cake cases and put teaspoonfuls of the mixture in each. Do not overfill.
5. Bake in a preheated oven for 12-15 minutes, until firm to the touch. Leave to cool.
6. Break the chocolate into a bowl over a saucepan of hot water, until the chocolate has melted.
7. Spread a layer of chocolate evenly over each cake. Leave to set.

SIMNEL CAKE

Makes one 20 cm (8 inch) cake
175 g (6 oz) butter or margarine
175 g (6 oz) caster sugar
3 eggs
450 g (1lb) mixed dried fruit
50 g (2 oz) glacé cherries, halved
3 tablespoons sherry or milk
225 g (8 oz) plain flour
2 teaspoons mixed spice
1 teaspoon baking powder
450 g (1 lb) marzipan
1 egg yolk, beaten
sugar-frosted flowers, to decorate (optional)

Preparation time: 30 minutes
Cooking time: 2½–2¾ hours
Oven: 160°C, 325°F, Gas Mark 3;
**   200°C, 400°F, Gas Mark 6**

Simnel cake was originally made by girls in Shrewsbury to give to their mothers as a gift on Mothering Sunday.

1. Grease and line a 20 cm (8 inch) round cake tin.
2. Place the butter or margarine and sugar in a bowl. Beat with a wooden spoon for 10 minutes or in a mixer for 5 minutes, until light and fluffy.
3. Beat in the eggs, a little at a time. Stir in the dried fruit, glacé cherries and sherry or milk.
4. Sift the flour, spice and baking powder into the bowl and fold in lightly using a metal spoon.
5. Roll out half the marzipan to a 20 cm (8 inch) round. Place half the cake mixture into the prepared tin. Smooth over the top and cover with the round of marzipan. Top with the remaining cake mixture, smoothing it with the back of a spoon.
6. Bake in a preheated oven for 2¼–2½ hours until the cake is deep golden brown and springs back when pressed with the fingers.
7. Leave to cool in the tin. When cold, turn out and remove the paper.
8. Roll out the remaining marzipan to fit the top of the cake. Brush the cake with a little of the egg yolk and place the marzipan on top. Mark the top of the cake in a lattice design with a knife and brush with the remaining egg yolk.
9. Place the cake on a baking sheet and bake in the oven at the higher temperature for 7–10 minutes until the marzipan is lightly browned.
10. If wished, decorate with a small posy of sugar-frosted flowers and a gold ribbon.

Simnel cake

Glazed nut loaf

GLAZED NUT LOAF

Makes one 1 kg (2 lb) loaf
100 g (4 oz) butter
100 g (4 oz) soft light brown sugar
2 eggs, beaten
100 g (4 oz) finely chopped mixed nuts
8 tablespoons milk
225 g (8 oz) self-raising flour
2 teaspoons ground cinnamon
25 g (1 oz) whole nuts, to decorate
1 tablespoon warmed honey, to glaze

Preparation time: 20 minutes
Cooking time: 50–55 minutes
Oven: 180°C, 350°F, Gas Mark 4

1. Grease and bottom-line a 1 kg (2 lb) loaf tin.
2. Place the butter and sugar in a bowl. Beat with a wooden spoon for 10 minutes, or in a mixer for 5 minutes, until light and fluffy.
3. Beat in the eggs, a little at a time.
4. Stir in the nuts and milk. Sift the flour and cinnamon into the bowl, then fold in lightly using a metal spoon.
5. Turn the mixture into the prepared tin and smooth over the top.
6. Arrange a cluster of whole nuts along the centre of the loaf, then place the tin on a baking sheet.
7. Bake in a preheated oven for 50–55 minutes, until the cake is deep golden brown and springs back when pressed with the fingers.
8. Cool in the tin for 5 minutes, then turn out and cool on a wire tray. Brush with the warmed honey.

CARIBBEAN CAKE

Makes one 1 kg (2 lb) loaf
1 × 225 g (8 oz) can pineapple slices, drained
100 g (4 oz) butter or margarine
100 g (4 oz) soft light brown sugar
2 eggs, beaten
100 g (4 oz) sultanas
3 tablespoons dark rum or milk
225 g (8 oz) self-raising flour
2 tablespoons demerara sugar, for sprinkling

Preparation time: 20 minutes
Cooking time: 1½–1¾ hours
Oven: 160°C, 325°F, Gas Mark 3

1. Grease and bottom-line a 1 kg (2 lb) loaf tin.
2. Finely chop the pineapple slices.
3. Place the butter and sugar in a bowl. Beat with a wooden spoon for 10 minutes, or in a mixer for 5 minutes, until light and fluffy.
4. Beat in the eggs, a little at a time.
5. Stir in two-thirds of the chopped pineapple, the sultanas and rum or milk. Add the flour and fold in lightly with a metal spoon until evenly mixed.
6. Turn the mixture into the prepared tin. Smooth the top of the cake and sprinkle with the reserved pineapple. Sprinkle the demerara sugar over the top.
7. Bake in a preheated oven for 1½–1¾ hours until the cake is golden brown and springs back when pressed with the fingers.
8. Cool in the tin for 5 minutes, then turn out and cool on a wire tray. To store, wrap in greaseproof paper, then foil and it will keep for up to 2 weeks.

PEACH UPSIDE-DOWN CAKE

Serves 6
25 g (1 oz) butter
50 g (2 oz) soft brown sugar
1 × 425 g (15 oz) can peach slices, drained
1 glacé cherry
100 g (4 oz) butter or margarine
100 g (4 oz) caster sugar
2 eggs, beaten
100 g (4 oz) self-raising flour
single or double cream, to serve

Preparation time: 20 minutes
Cooking time: 45–50 minutes
Oven: 180°C, 350°F, Gas Mark 4

1. Grease and bottom-line a 1.5 litre (2½ pint) charlotte tin.
2. Melt the 25 g (1 oz) of butter and pour it into the base of the prepared charlotte tin. Sprinkle the brown sugar over the top.
3. Arrange the peach slices in the base of the tin, radiating from the centre. Place a cherry in the centre.
4. Place the butter or margarine and caster sugar in a bowl. Beat with a wooden spoon for 10 minutes, or in a mixer for 5 minutes, until light and fluffy.
5. Beat in the eggs, a little at a time.
6. Add the flour and fold in lightly with a metal spoon until evenly mixed.
7. Place spoonsful of the cake mixture over the peaches in the tin. Smooth the top with the back of a metal spoon.
8. Bake in a preheated oven for 45–50 minutes until the cake is golden brown and springs back when pressed with the fingers.
9. Turn the cake out upside-down on to a serving plate and serve warm with cream.

JUMBLES

Makes about 32
100 g (4 oz) butter or margarine
100 g (4 oz) soft light brown sugar
1 egg, beaten
225 g (8 oz) self-raising flour
25 g (1 oz) caster sugar
1 teaspoon ground cinnamon

Preparation time: 20 minutes
Cooking time: 15–20 minutes
Oven: 180°C, 350°F, Gas Mark 4

Coffee kisses; Jumbles

1. Place the butter or margarine and sugar in a bowl. Beat with a wooden spoon for 10 minutes, or in a mixer for 5 minutes, until light and fluffy.
2. Beat in the egg, a little at a time.
3. Add the flour and fold in lightly with a metal spoon to form a firm dough.
4. Pull off small pieces of the dough and, using your fingers, roll into thin sausage shapes, about 13 cm (5 inches) long. Shape the dough into knots, rounds and 'S' shapes. Place on greased baking sheets, leaving space for them to spread.
5. Mix together the sugar and cinnamon and sprinkle over the biscuits.
6. Bake the biscuits in a preheated oven for 15–20 minutes until pale golden, then transfer to a wire tray and leave to cool.

COFFEE KISSES

Makes about 15
100 g (4 oz) butter or margarine
50 g (2 oz) caster sugar
125 g (5 oz) self-raising flour
3 tablespoons strong black coffee
Icing:
50 g (2 oz) butter, softened
100 g (4 oz) icing sugar, sifted
1 tablespoon strong black coffee
icing sugar, for dusting

Preparation time: 20 minutes
Cooking time: 10 minutes
Oven: 190°C, 375°F, Gas Mark 5

1. Place the butter or margarine and sugar in a bowl. Beat with a wooden spoon for 10 minutes, or in a mixer for 5 minutes, until light and fluffy.
2. Add the flour and coffee and mix to a stiff dough.
3. Place the mixture in a piping bag, fitted with a large star tube. Pipe an even number of small stars of the mixture, a little apart, on a greased baking sheet. The mixture will make about 30 stars.
4. Bake in a preheated oven for 10 minutes, until just beginning to colour. Cool on the baking sheet for 5 minutes, then remove and leave to cool completely on a wire tray.
5. To make the icing, beat together the butter, icing sugar and coffee until light and creamy.
6. Sandwich 2 stars together with a little icing, then dust with icing sugar.

RUBBING IN, ROLLING & FOLDING

SCONES

Makes 8–10
200 g (8 oz) self-raising flour
½ teaspoon salt
50 g (2 oz) butter or margarine
25 g (1 oz) caster sugar
150 ml (¼ pint) milk
milk, to glaze

Preparation time: 15 minutes
Cooking time: 12–15 minutes
Oven: 220°C, 425°F, Gas Mark 7

1. Place the flour and salt in a bowl. Add the butter or margarine, cut into pieces, and rub into the flour with the fingertips until the mixture resembles fine breadcrumbs.
2. Stir in the sugar. Add the milk and mix lightly to a soft dough.
3. Turn out on to a floured surface and knead lightly. Do not overhandle: the less the mixture is handled, the lighter the result.
4. Roll out to 1 cm (½ inch) thickness and cut into rounds with a 6 cm (2½ inch) fluted pastry cutter.
5. Place the scones on a baking sheet and brush with milk. Bake in a preheated oven for 12–15 minutes, until risen and golden brown.

Variations:
Fruit scones: Add 50 g (2 oz) dried fruit to the rubbed in mixture, before adding the milk.
Spicy scones: Add 2 teaspoons mixed spice to the flour. Replace the caster sugar with soft dark brown sugar.
Wheatmeal scones: Replace half the flour with wheatmeal flour and add 2 teaspoons baking powder. Add an extra 2 tablespoons milk.
Cheese scones: Add 75 g (3 oz) finely grated mature Cheddar cheese, 1 teaspoon dry mustard and a pinch of cayenne pepper to the rubbed in mixture. Omit the sugar and use a plain pastry cutter.
Yogurt and honey scones: Replace the milk with 150 ml (¼ pint) plain unsweetened yogurt and use 3 tablespoons clear honey instead of the sugar, adding the honey at the same time as you add the yogurt. Roll out the dough to a 20 cm (8 inch) round and cut it into 8 wedges. Place the scones on a baking sheet, brush with milk and sprinkle with demerara sugar. Bake as above.

SINGIN' HINNY

Makes 8 wedges
225 g (8 oz) self-raising flour
½ teaspoon salt
50 g (2 oz) lard
50 g (2 oz) caster sugar
75 g (3 oz) currants
1 egg, beaten
6 tablespoons milk

Preparation time: 10 minutes
Cooking time: 20 minutes

This griddle scone gets its name from the sound it makes while being cooked. It burns easily so be sure to keep it on a low heat.

1. Place the flour and salt in a bowl. Add the lard, cut into pieces, and rub into the flour until the mixture resembles fine breadcrumbs.
2. Stir in the sugar and currants. Add the beaten egg and milk and mix to a soft dough.
3. Turn out on to a lightly floured surface and knead lightly. Roll or press out to a 20 cm (8 inch) round.
4. Heat a griddle or heavy-based frying pan, which has been lightly greased with oil.
5. Cook the cake over a low heat for 10 minutes, then carefully turn it over and cook for a further 10 minutes.
6. Slide the cake on to a plate and cut into 8 wedges. Serve warm, split and buttered.

Light handling is the secret to light results when making this griddle cake. Add the egg and milk in one go and mix just sufficiently to bind the mixture. Knead it very briefly and don't worry if there are a few cracks in the dough. It is a homely cake and will look very welcoming cut into wedges and oozing with melted butter.

Singin' Hinny; Scones with Fruit and Wheatmeal variations

LEMON TARTS M

Makes 18–20
25 g (1 oz) fresh white breadcrumbs
finely grated rind of 2 lemons
2 tablespoons lemon juice
50 g (2 oz) butter, diced
120 ml (4 fl oz) milk
25 g (1 oz) caster sugar
25 g (1 oz) semolina
2 eggs, beaten
few drops vanilla essence
Shortcrust pastry:
200 g (8 oz) plain flour
pinch of salt
50 g (2 oz) lard
50 g (2 oz) butter or margarine
2 tablespoons cold water

Preparation time: 25 minutes
Cooking time: 30–35 minutes
Oven: 190°C, 375°F, Gas mark 5;
       160°C, 325°F, Gas Mark 3

PLUM AND MALLOW PIE

Serves 6–8
150 g (6 oz) wheatmeal flour
pinch of salt
75 g (3 oz) lard and butter, mixed in equal amounts
2 tablespoons cold water
750 g (1½ lb) plums, stoned
100 g (4 oz) marshmallows
50 g (2 oz) caster sugar
milk, to glaze

Preparation time: 20 minutes
Cooking time: 30 minutes
Oven: 200°C, 400°F, Gas Mark 6

1. Place the flour and salt in a bowl. Add the fats, cut into pieces, and rub into the flour until the mixture resembles fine breadcrumbs. Add the water and mix to a firm dough.
2. Knead the dough until smooth on a lightly floured surface. Wrap in cling film and leave to rest.
3. Mix together the plums, marshmallows and sugar. Pile into a 1.5 litre (2½ pint) pie dish.
4. Roll out the pastry to 5 cm (2 inches) larger than the pie dish top. Cut off a 3 cm (1 inch) strip all round to line the edge of the dish. Brush with water.
5. Lift the rest of the pastry on to the pie, pressing the edges to seal. Trim. Brush with milk.
6. Place a baking sheet and bake in a preheated oven for 30 minutes until golden brown. Serve warm.

1. To make the filling, place the breadcrumbs, lemon rind, juice and butter in a basin. Heat the milk and pour over. Leave for 10 minutes. Stir in the sugar, semolina, beaten eggs and vanilla.
2. To make the pastry, place the flour and salt in a bowl. Add the lard and butter or margarine, cut into small pieces.
3. Rub the fat into the flour using the fingertips, until the mixture resembles fine breadcrumbs. Shake the bowl to bring any lumps to the surface.
4. Add the water and mix with a round-ended knife, until the dough begins to hold together. Draw together with one hand, pressing the dough around the bowl to collect any stray bits.
5. Turn the dough out on to a lightly floured surface. Knead lightly, until smooth and silky.
6. Roll out the pastry thinly using short forward strokes, turning the pastry between each rolling. Do not turn the dough over.
7. Using a 9 cm (3½ inch) fluted cutter, cut into rounds. Draw up trimmings and roll out as before.
8. Line patty tins with the pastry rounds. Put a little filling into each and bake in a preheated oven for 20 minutes, then reduce the temperature and continue cooking for 10–15 minutes, until the pastry is golden and the filling has risen. Serve warm or cold.

Rubbing in the fat

Drawing the dough together

Kneading lightly

Rolling out

Covering a pie

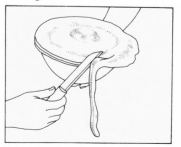

Trimming the edges

Pear and hazelnut tart

PEAR AND HAZELNUT TART

Serves 6–8
150 g (6 oz) plain flour
1 tablespoon caster sugar
75 g (3 oz) butter, diced
25 g (1 oz) ground hazelnuts
1 egg yolk
2 teaspoons water
Filling:
2–3 medium pears
75 g (3 oz) caster sugar
1 egg
25 g (1 oz) plain flour
150 ml (¼ pint) milk
3 tablespoons brandy (optional)

Preparation time: 30 minutes
Cooking time: 35 minutes
Oven: 220°C, 425°F, Gas Mark 7;
      190°C, 375°F, Gas Mark 5

1. To make the pastry, place the flour, sugar, butter, hazelnuts, egg yolk and water in a bowl. Work the ingredients together with one hand to form a firm dough.

2. Turn out on to a lightly floured surface and knead lightly. Roll out and line a 23 cm (9 inch) flan tin.
3. To make the filling, peel, halve and core the pears, then with cut side down, slice thinly lengthways. Place in the flan case radiating from the centre.
4. Sprinkle the pears with 25 g (1 oz) of the sugar and bake in a preheated oven for 15 minutes until the pastry is golden brown.
5. Beat together the remaining sugar, the egg and flour until smooth. Beat in the milk and brandy (if using), until evenly mixed.
6. Pour the custard over the pears in the pastry case. Reduce the oven temperature and return the tart to the oven for a further 20 minutes, until the filling is set. Serve warm or cold.

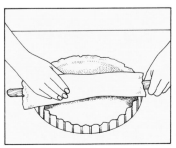
Lining the tin with pastry

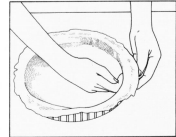
Easing pastry into the sides

GYPSY TART

Serves 6–8
150 g (6 oz) plain flour
pinch of salt
75 g (3 oz) lard and butter, mixed in equal amounts
2 tablespoons cold water
1 × 175 g (6 oz) can evaporated milk
150 g (6 oz) natural dark brown sugar

Preparation time: 20 minutes
Cooking time: 30 minutes
Oven: 200°C, 400°F, Gas Mark 6

This butterscotch flavour tart reminds me of my schooldays when it was my favourite pudding. It's important to use natural sugar to make the filling set.

1. Place the flour and salt in a bowl. Add the fat, cut into pieces, and rub into the flour until the mixture resembles fine breadcrumbs. Add the water and mix to a firm dough.
2. Turn out the pastry on to a lightly floured surface and knead lightly.
3. Roll out and line a 23 cm (9 inch) pie plate or flan tin. Bake blind in a preheated oven for 20 minutes.
4. Place the milk and sugar in a bowl. Whisk with an electric whisk for 5 minutes until light and thick.
5. Pour into the pastry case and bake for a further 10 minutes. Remove from the oven and allow to cool, until the filling is completely set. Serve cold.

BANANA RAISIN BREAD

Makes one 1 kg (2 lb) loaf
225 g (8 oz) self-raising flour
½ teaspoon salt
100 g (4 oz) butter or margarine
175 g (6 oz) soft dark brown sugar
75 g (3 oz) raisins
2 ripe bananas
½ teaspoon vanilla essence
1 egg, beaten
3 tablespoons milk

Preparation time: 15 minutes
Cooking time: 1½ hours
Oven: 160°C, 325°F, Gas Mark 3

1. Line the bottom of a 1 kg (2 lb) loaf tin with greaseproof paper and grease the tin all over.
2. Place the flour and salt in a bowl. Add the butter or margarine, cut into pieces, and rub into the flour until the mixture resembles fine breadcrumbs.
3. Stir in the sugar and raisins. Mash the bananas with a fork and add to the mixture with the vanilla essence, beaten egg and milk. Beat until well mixed.
4. Turn the mixture into the prepared tin and smooth the top with the back of a spoon.
5. Place the tin on a baking sheet and bake in a preheated oven for 1½ hours, until the cake is golden brown and springs back when pressed with the fingers.
6. Leave in the tin for 10 minutes, then turn out and cool on a wire tray. Serve sliced and buttered.

Try to buy natural brown sugars for your baking, that is, those that state the country of origin on the packet. The flavour is appreciably better and the sugar moister. If you find it goes solid, place it in a stoppered jar with a crust of bread. It should soften in a day.

Banana raisin bread; Cherry bumpers

CHERRY BUMPERS

Makes 12

350 g (12 oz) cherries, stoned
50 g (2 oz) sugar
1 tablespoon water
200 g (8 oz) Shortcrust Pastry (page 24)
milk, to glaze

Preparation time: 25 minutes, plus cooling
Cooking time: 20–25 minutes
Oven: 200°C, 400°F, Gas Mark 6

When cherries are out of season use a can of pie filling and omit step 1.

1. Place the cherries, sugar and water in a saucepan. Cook gently, stirring occasionally, until the cherries are softened, about 5 minutes. Leave to cool.
2. Roll out the pastry and cut into twelve 10 cm (4 inch) rounds. Divide the cherries between the rounds and damp the edges of the pastry.
3. Draw up the pastry over the filling, pressing the edges to seal. Flute the join by pinching with the fingers.
4. Place the bumpers on a baking sheet and brush with milk. Bake in a preheated oven for 20–25 minutes until golden brown. Serve warm or cold.

Variation:
Apple and sultana bumpers: Peel, core and chop 1 large cooking apple. Cook with 50 g (2 oz) sugar and 3 tablespoons water until soft. Stir in 25 g (1 oz) sultanas.

MINCEMEAT AND APPLE SLICE

Makes 12
300 g (12 oz) plain flour
½ teaspoon salt
75 g (3 oz) lard
75 g (3 oz) butter or margarine
3–4 tablespoons cold water
Filling:
225 g (8 oz) cooking apple
2 teaspoons finely grated orange rind
450 g (1 lb) mincemeat
caster sugar, for sprinkling

Preparation time: 20 minutes
Cooking time: 35–40 minutes
Oven: 200°C, 400°F, Gas Mark 6

1. Place the flour and salt in a bowl. Add the lard and butter or margarine, cut into pieces, and rub into the flour until the mixture resembles fine bread-crumbs. Add the water and mix to a firm dough.
2. Turn out on to a lightly floured surface and knead lightly. Roll out two-thirds of the pastry and line a 33 cm × 23 cm (13 inch × 9 inch) Swiss roll tin.
3. Peel, quarter and core the apple. Coarsely grate it into a bowl. Add the orange rind and mincemeat and mix well.
4. Spread the filling evenly over the pastry case. Roll out the reserved pastry and cut into long thin strips. Twist the strips and arrange in a lattice design over the filling. Damp the ends and press to stick on to the pastry base.
5. Bake in a preheated oven for 35–40 minutes until the pastry is golden. Sprinkle with caster sugar and cut into slices to serve.

ECCLES CAKES M

Makes 10–12
Rough Puff Pastry
200 g (8 oz) plain flour
½ teaspoon salt
75 g (3 oz) lard
75 g (3 oz) butter or margarine
2 teaspoons lemon juice
8 tablespoons cold water
Filling:
25 g (1 oz) butter
150 g (6 oz) currants
25 g (1 oz) cut mixed peel
50 g (2 oz) soft dark brown sugar
2 teaspoons mixed spice
egg white, to glaze
caster sugar, for sprinkling

Preparation time: 30 minutes, plus chilling
Cooking time: 25 minutes
Oven: 220°C, 425°F, Gas Mark 7

1. To make the rough puff pastry, place the flour and salt in a bowl. Cut the fats into small pieces and toss in the flour to coat them.
2. Add the lemon juice and cold water and mix lightly with a round-ended knife to make a soft lumpy dough. Place the dough on a floured surface and shape into a square.
3. Roll out the dough, using short forward strokes, to an oblong 36 cm × 13 cm (15 inches × 5 inches).
4. Fold up the bottom third of the dough and the top third down to cover it. Press the edges together to seal. Give the dough a quarter turn and roll and fold as before. Sprinkle the dough with the flour and place in a plastic bag. Chill for 20 minutes.
5. Repeat rolling and folding twice more and chill for a further 30 minutes before using.
6. To make the filling, melt the butter in a saucepan, add the currants, mixed peel, sugar and spice and mix well.
7. Roll out the dough 5 mm (¼ inch) thick and cut into ten to twelve 10 cm (4 inch) rounds. Divide the filling between the rounds. Damp the pastry edges and draw up over the filling, pinching the edges together to seal. Turn the pastries over and roll out again to 7½ cm (3 inch) rounds.
8. Place the pastries on a baking sheet and make 3 slits in the centre of each. Brush with lightly beaten egg white and sprinkle with caster sugar.
9. Bake in a preheated oven for 25 minutes, until the pastry is risen and golden brown.

Mixing with a knife

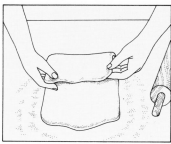
Folding up bottom third

Folding down top third

Pressing the edges to seal

APRICOT AND RAISIN ENVELOPES

Makes 12
75 g (3 oz) dried apricots, chopped
75 g (3 oz) seedless raisins
300 ml (½ pint) water
75 g (3 oz) ground almonds
200 g (8 oz) Rough Puff Pastry (see left)
milk, to glaze

Preparation time: 40 minutes, plus chilling
Cooking time: 25 minutes
Oven: 220°C, 425°F, Gas Mark 7

1. Place the apricots, raisins and water in a saucepan. Bring to the boil, reduce the heat, cover and cook gently for 20 minutes, until soft and pulpy.
2. Remove from the heat and stir in the ground almonds. Leave to cool.
3. Roll out the pastry and trim to a 40 cm × 30 cm (16 inch × 12 inch) oblong. Cut into twelve 10 cm (4 inch) squares.
4. Pile the filling into the centre of each square. Damp the edges of the pastry. Draw up the corners to the centre, pressing the edges to seal. Flute the edges.
5. Place the envelopes on a baking sheet and brush with milk. Bake in a preheated oven for 25 minutes, until golden brown.

FROM THE LEFT: Eccles cakes; Apricot and raisin envelopes; Mincemeat and apple slice

CHERRY BASKET

Serves 6–8

225g (8 oz) Puff Pastry (opposite)
300 ml (½ pint) double cream, whipped until stiff
450 g (1 lb) cherries, stoned, or 1 × 425 g (15 oz) can stoned cherries, drained
25 g (1 oz) toasted flaked almonds

Preparation time: 45 minutes
Cooking time: 15 minutes
Oven: 220°C, 425°F, Gas Mark 7

Cherry basket; Custard slice

1. Divide the pastry into 3. Roll out each piece and cut into 23 cm (9 inch) rounds. Remove the centre from 2 of the rounds, using a 10 cm (4 inch) pastry cutter.
2. Cut 8 pastry leaves from the trimmings. Place the pastry round, rings and leaves on damp baking sheets and bake in a preheated oven for 15 minutes. Cool the pastry on a wire tray.
3. Place 2 tablespoonsful of the cream in a piping bag fitted with a large star tube and reserve.
4. Spread one-third of the remaining cream around the edge of the pastry round. Scatter over it half the cherries.
5. Place 1 of the pastry rings on top and spread with half of the remaining cream. Reserve 4 cherries and scatter the remainder over the top. Cover with the remaining pastry ring.
6. Spread the remaining cream over the top and sprinkle with the flaked almonds. Pipe 4 whirls of cream over the top and decorate each with a cherry and 2 pastry leaves. Serve immediately.

CUSTARD SLICE M

Makes 10 slices
225 g (8 oz) plain or white bread flour
½ teaspoon salt
225 g (8 oz) butter
2 teaspoons lemon juice
8 tablespoons cold water
Custard:
1 egg
50 g (2 oz) caster sugar
40 g (1½ oz) plain flour
300 ml (½ pint) milk
vanilla essence
25 g (1 oz) butter
4 tablespoons strawberry jam
icing sugar, for sprinkling

Preparation time: 40 minutes, plus chilling
Cooking time: 15–20 minutes
Oven: 220°C, 425°F, Gas Mark 7

1. To make the puff pastry, place the flour and salt in a bowl. Add a small piece of the 225 g (8 oz) butter and rub into the flour with the fingertips.
2. Add the lemon juice and water and mix to a soft dough. Turn out the dough on to a lightly floured surface and knead until smooth and silky. Shape the dough into a square, place in a plastic bag and chill for 20 minutes.
3. Place the rest of the butter on a large flat plate and soften with a round-ended knife. Shape into an oblong 13 cm × 10 cm (5 inches × 4 inches), making sure that the top and sides are flat and the corners square. Chill while you roll out the dough.
4. Roll out the dough using short forward strokes to an oblong 36 cm × 13 cm (15 inches × 5 inches). Place the block of butter lengthways in the centre.
5. Fold the bottom third of the dough up and the top third down to cover the fat. Press the edges to seal.
6. Give the dough a quarter turn and flatten slightly with a rolling pin. Roll out and fold the dough as before.
7. Return the dough to the plastic bag and chill for a further 20 minutes, until firm.
8. Repeat the rolling and folding twice more. Chill the dough for another 30 minutes before using.
9. Roll out the dough to an oblong 30 cm × 36 cm (12 inches × 15 inches). Cut into 3 across the width.
10. Place the 3 strips on a damp baking sheet and bake in a preheated oven for 15 minutes, until well risen and golden brown. Cool on a wire tray.
11. To make the custard, beat together the egg, sugar and flour with 2 tablespoons of the milk, until smooth. Heat the remaining milk and stir into the egg mixture.
12. Return the mixture to the pan and cook gently, stirring until thickened and smooth. Cook for 2 minutes, stirring all the time.
13. Remove from the heat and beat in a few drops of vanilla and the butter. Cover with cling-film and leave until cold.
14. Place 1 pastry strip on a serving plate. Spread a layer of jam over it and cover with half the custard.
15. Place the second piece of pastry on top, cover with the remaining jam and custard and top with the third pastry strip. Dust with sifted icing sugar. Cut into slices with a serrated knife to serve.

Softening the butter

Positioning the butter

CREAMY FRUIT JALOUSIE

Serves 6

175 g (6 oz) butter
225 g (8 oz) plain flour
½ teaspoon salt
8 tablespoons water
150 ml (¼ pint) cold custard
150 ml (¼ pint) double cream
350 g (12 oz) mixed fresh or frozen fruit e.g. grape halves, peach slices, banana slices, raspberries, strawberries
1 tablespoon apricot jam

Preparation time: 35 minutes, plus freezing and chilling
Cooking time: 20 minutes
Oven: 220°C, 425°F, Gas Mark 7

1. To make quick flaky pastry, wrap the butter in foil and place in the freezer or frozen-food compartment for 30 minutes.
2. Place the flour and salt in a bowl. Grate the butter into the flour, peeling back the foil and dipping the block into flour as you go. Mix the fat into the flour evenly with a knife.
3. Add the water and mix to a soft dough. Wrap in cling film and chill for 20 minutes.
4. Roll out the pastry to an oblong 25 cm × 15 cm (10 inches × 6 inches). Fold in half lengthways and cut an oblong out of the centre, leaving a 2 cm (1 inch) border. Roll out the centre piece to an oblong 25 cm × 15 cm (10 inches × 6 inches). Damp the edges. Open out the reserved pastry and place on top of the oblong.
5. Place the oblong pastry 'basket' on a damp baking sheet. Flake and flute the edges.
6. Prick the base of the pastry and bake in a preheated oven for 20 minutes, until risen and golden brown. Cool on a wire tray.
7. Whisk the custard until lighter in colour. Whisk the cream until thick, then whisk into the custard.
8. Spread the creamy custard over the pastry base. Arrange the fruit in rows over the top.
9. Heat the jam with 1 tablespoon of water. Press through a sieve and cool slightly. Brush over the fruit to glaze. Serve immediately.

ST CATHERINE'S CAKES

Makes 24
350 g (12 oz) plain flour
½ teaspoon bicarbonate of soda
1 teaspoon mixed spice
25 g (1 oz) ground almonds
225 g (8 oz) caster sugar
225 g (8 oz) butter or margarine
50 g (2 oz) currants
1 egg, lightly beaten
25 g (1 oz) granulated sugar

Preparation time: 20 minutes
Cooking time: 12–15 minutes
Oven: 200°C, 400°F, Gas Mark 6

1. Sift the flour, bicarbonate of soda and spice into a bowl. Stir in the almonds and caster sugar.
2. Add the butter or margarine, cut into pieces, and rub in until the mixture resembles fine breadcrumbs. Stir in the currants.
3. Add the beaten egg and mix to a firm dough. Turn out on to a floured surface and knead lightly.
4. Roll out the dough to an oblong 30 cm × 20 cm (12 inches × 8 inches). Brush with water and sprinkle with the granulated sugar. Cut into strips 1 cm × 20 cm (½ inch × 8 inches).
5. Form each strip into a coil, then place on greased baking sheets, leaving room for each coil to spread.
6. Bake in a preheated oven for 12–15 minutes, until light golden. Cool slightly, then remove from the baking sheet and finish cooling on a wire tray. Serve warm or cold.

APPLE SPICE CAKE

Makes one 20 cm (8 inch) cake
225 g (8 oz) self-raising flour
1 teaspoon ground cinnamon
½ teaspoon grated nutmeg
150 g (5 oz) butter
100 g (4 oz) caster sugar
200 g (8 oz) apple purée
2 eggs, beaten
Topping:
25 g (1 oz) chopped nuts
1 teaspoon ground cinnamon
25 g (1 oz) demerara sugar

Preparation time: 15–20 minutes
Cooking time: 1¼–1½ hours
Oven: 190°C, 375°F, Gas Mark 5

CRUNCHY FRUIT BARS

Makes 16
225 g (8 oz) dried fruit salad (e.g. peaches, pears, apples, bananas, dates, figs), chopped
300 ml (½ pint) water
150 ml (¼ pint) orange juice
150 g (6 oz) plain flour
100 g (4 oz) semolina
100 g (4 oz) butter or margarine
75 g (3 oz) caster sugar
granulated sugar, for sprinkling

Preparation time: 15 minutes
Cooking time: about 1 hour
Oven: 190°C, 375°F, Gas Mark 5

1. Place the dried fruit, water and orange juice in a saucepan. Bring to the boil, then reduce the heat, cover and cook gently for 30 minutes. Leave to cool.
2. Place the flour and semolina in a bowl. Add the butter or margarine, cut into pieces, and rub in until the mixture resembles fine breadcrumbs. Stir in the caster sugar.
3. Sprinkle half the crumble evenly over the base of a 28 cm × 18 cm (11 inch × 7 inch) shallow tin. Carefully spread the fruit over the top and sprinkle with the remaining crumble. Press down lightly.
4. Bake in a preheated oven for 30–35 minutes, until pale golden. Sprinkle with granulated sugar and leave in the tin until cold. Cut in half down the length, then into 8 across to make into bars.

Variation:
Replace the dried fruit salad with chopped dates and add the rind and juice of 1 lemon.

A jar of apple sauce works very well in this cake, if time is short.

1. Grease and bottom-line a 20 cm (8 inch) cake tin.
2. Place the flour and spices in a bowl. Add the butter, cut into pieces, and rub into the flour, until the mixture resembles fine breadcrumbs.
3. Stir in the sugar. Add the apple purée and beaten eggs and mix to a soft consistency.
4. Pour into the prepared tin and level the top.
5. Mix together the topping ingredients and sprinkle over the cake. Bake in a preheated oven for 1¼–1½ hours, until the cake is golden brown and springs back when pressed with the fingers.
6. Leave in the tin for 10 minutes then turn out and cool on a wire tray.

FROM THE LEFT: St Catherine's cakes; Crunchy fruit bars

GRASMERE GINGERBREAD

Makes 12

225 g (8 oz) wheatmeal flour
½ teaspoon bicarbonate of soda
2 teaspoons ground ginger
175 g (6 oz) butter
175 g (6 oz) moist light brown sugar
1 tablespoon golden syrup
granulated sugar, for sprinkling

Preparation time: 15 minutes
Cooking time: 35 minutes
Oven: 160°C, 325°F, Gas Mark 3

These spicy biscuits are given out to the children of Grasmere in Cumbria during the annual rush-bearing ceremony.

1. Place the flour, bicarbonate of soda and ginger in a bowl. Add the butter, cut into pieces, and rub into the flour until the mixture resembles fine breadcrumbs. Stir in the sugar.
2. Drizzle the syrup into the mixture, stirring all the time, until evenly mixed.
3. Sprinkle the mixture evenly over a 33 cm × 23 cm (13 inch × 9 inch) shallow oblong tin. Press the mixture down lightly with the back of a metal spoon.
4. Bake in a preheated oven for 35 minutes until crisp and golden.
5. Sprinkle with the sugar, then cut in half down the length and into 3 across. Mark each square to make a line through the centre, using a knife. Allow to cool in the tin. When cold, remove and break each piece in half down the marked line.

ROCK CAKES

Makes 12
100 g (4 oz) self-raising flour
100 g (4 oz) wheatmeal flour
1 teaspoon baking powder
½ teaspoon salt
½ teaspoon grated nutmeg
100 g (4 oz) butter or margarine
75 g (3 oz) caster sugar
50 g (2 oz) sultanas
1 egg, beaten
1–2 tablespoons milk

Preparation time: 15 minutes
Cooking time: 12–15 minutes
Oven: 230°C, 450°F, Gas Mark 8

1. Place the flours, baking powder, salt and nutmeg in a bowl. Add the butter or margarine, cut into pieces, and rub into the flour until the mixture resembles fine breadcrumbs.
2. Stir in the sugar and sultanas. Add the beaten egg and mix until stiff, adding the milk if necessary.
3. Using 2 forks place portions of the mixture in 12 rough heaps on a greased baking sheet.
4. Bake in a preheated oven for 12–15 minutes, until rich golden brown. Remove from the baking sheet and cool on a wire tray.

PEANUT BISCUITS

Makes about 50
275 g (10 oz) plain flour
½ teaspoon baking powder
½ teaspoon salt
½ teaspoon bicarbonate of soda
100 g (4 oz) margarine
225 g (8 oz) soft light brown sugar
100 g (4 oz) crunchy peanut butter
2 eggs, beaten

Preparation time: 15 minutes
Cooking time: 12–15 minutes
Oven: 200°C, 400°F, Gas Mark 6

1. Sift the flour, baking powder, salt and bicarbonate of soda into a bowl. Add the margarine, cut into pieces, and rub into the flour until the mixture resembles fine breadcrumbs.
2. Stir in the sugar. Add the peanut butter and beaten eggs and mix to a soft dough.
3. Form the dough into small balls, about 3 cm (1 inch) across and place a little apart on greased baking sheets. Mark each biscuit by pressing the surface with a fork to make a criss-cross pattern.
4. Bake in a preheated oven for 12–15 minutes until risen. Remove and leave for 1 minute, then transfer to a wire tray to cool. Store in an airtight tin.

PITCAITHLY BANNOCK

Makes 16
150 g (6 oz) plain flour
25 g (1 oz) ground rice
100 g (4 oz) butter, cut into pieces
75 g (3 oz) caster sugar
25 g (1 oz) cut mixed peel
25 g (1 oz) unblanched almonds, finely chopped
1 tablespoon milk
caster sugar, for sprinkling

Preparation time: 15 minutes
Cooking time: 35 minutes
Oven: 160°C, 325°F, Gas Mark 3

1. Place the flour and ground rice in a bowl. Add the butter and rub in until the mixture resembles fine breadcrumbs. Stir in the sugar, peel and almonds.
2. Add the milk and work with the hands until the mixture clings together. Divide the mixture in half.
3. Knead one piece of dough until smooth. Place inside an 18 cm (7 inch) fluted flan ring on a baking sheet and press out evenly. Carefully remove the ring and repeat with the remaining dough.
4. Prick both rounds all over and bake in a preheated oven for 35 minutes until lightly coloured.
5. Leave for 5 minutes, then sprinkle with caster sugar and cut each round into 8. Cool on a wire tray.

NUT CHOC CHIP BISCUITS

Makes about 30
225 g (8 oz) plain flour
1 teaspoon baking powder
100 g (4 oz) margarine
150 g (5 oz) caster sugar
25 g (1 oz) toasted hazelnuts, finely chopped
25 g (1 oz) plain or milk chocolate, finely chopped
1 tablespoon black treacle
3 tablespoons milk

Preparation time: 20 minutes, plus chilling
Cooking time: 12–15 minutes
Oven: 190°C, 375°F, Gas Mark 5

1. Place the flour and baking powder in a bowl. Add the margarine, cut into pieces, and rub into the flour until the mixture resembles fine breadcrumbs.
2. Stir in the sugar, nuts and chocolate. Add the treacle and milk and mix to a firm dough. Turn out on to a floured surface and knead lightly.
3. Shape into a roll 5 cm (2 inches) thick and wrap in cling film. Chill for 30 minutes.
4. Cut the roll into thin slices and place a little apart on greased baking sheets. Bake in a preheated oven for 12–15 minutes, until beginning to colour.
5. Remove and leave the biscuits for 1 minute, then transfer to a wire tray to cool. Store in an airtight tin.

MELTING & WHISKING

BRANDY AND ORANGE GÂTEAU

Serves 6
2 eggs
50 g (2 oz) caster sugar
50 g (2 oz) plain flour
grated rind of 1 orange
1 quantity Barnstaple Gingerbread mixture (page 48)
300 ml (½ pint) double cream
3 tablespoons brandy

Preparation time: 40 minutes
Cooking time: about 30 minutes
Oven: 180°C, 350°F, Gas Mark 4

1. Grease and bottom-line two 18 cm (7 inch) sandwich cake tins.
2. Place the eggs and sugar in a bowl over hot water. (If using an electric whisk the hot water is unnecessary.) Whisk for about 5 minutes, until the mixture is light and thick and leaves a trail when the whisk is lifted from it.
3. Sift the flour into the bowl and fold lightly into the mixture with a metal spoon or the mixer blades. Add half the orange rind and fold in.
4. Divide the mixture between the 2 prepared tins. Shake the tins to level the mixture.
5. Bake in a preheated oven for 20 minutes, until light golden and firm to the touch.
6. Turn out the cakes and cool on a wire tray.
7. Make up the gingerbread mixture and bake as directed (page 48). While still warm, shape 6 biscuits into cone shapes.
8. When cold, break up the flat biscuits into small pieces. Whisk the cream and brandy until stiff. Stir in the remaining orange rind.
9. Place the cake on a serving plate and spread with a little cream. Sprinkle with the broken biscuits and place the other cake on top.
10. Spread the cream round the side of the cake and roll in the remaining broken biscuits to cover. Spread the top of the cake with a little cream. Place spoonfuls of the remaining cream in a piping bag fitted with a star tube.
11. Fill the cones with cream and place on top of the cake, radiating from the centre. Pipe cream rosettes round the edge of the cake and 1 in the centre.

APRICOT SPONGE [M]

Makes one 18 cm (7 inch) cake
2 eggs
50 g (2 oz) caster sugar
50 g (2 oz) plain flour
2 rounded tablespoons apricot jam
icing sugar, for sprinkling
150 ml (¼ pint) double or whipping cream, whipped

Preparation time: 15 minutes
Cooking time: 20 minutes
Oven: 180°C, 350°F, Gas Mark 4

1. Grease and bottom-line two 18 cm (7 inch) sandwich tins.
2. Place the eggs and caster sugar in a bowl over hot water. (If using an electric whisk the hot water is unnecessary.) Whisk for about 5 minutes, until the mixture is light and thick and leaves a trail when the whisk is lifted from it.
3. Sift the flour into the bowl. Fold it into the mixture lightly and carefully, using a metal spoon or the whisk blades, cutting through the mixture and turning it over until the flour is evenly mixed.
4. Divide the mixture between the 2 prepared tins. Shake the tins to level the mixture.
5. Bake in a preheated oven for 20 minutes, until lightly browned and firm to the touch.
6. Loosen the edges of the cakes with fingertips or a plastic spatula, then turn out, remove paper and cool on a wire tray.
7. Place 1 cake on a serving plate. Spread with the jam and then the whipped cream. Place the other cake on top. Sprinkle with sieved icing sugar.

> To avoid a last minute panic, have all your ingredients weighed and ready before you start to make a whisked cake. Try to use eggs that have been at room temperature for an hour or so, they will whisk better to make a lighter cake.

MOCHA PRALINE GÂTEAU

Makes one 20 cm (8 inch) cake
3 eggs
75 g (3 oz) caster sugar
50 g (2 oz) plain flour
25 g (1 oz) cocoa powder
1 teaspoon instant coffee
Icing:
100 g (4 oz) plain chocolate
2 egg whites
100 g (4 oz) icing sugar, sifted
150 g (5 oz) butter
Praline:
100 g (4 oz) caster sugar
50 g (2 oz) blanched almonds
chocolate curls, to decorate

Preparation time: 45 minutes
Cooking time: 35–40 minutes
Oven: 180°C, 350°F, Gas Mark 4

1. Grease and bottom-line two 20 cm (8 inch) sandwich cake tins.
2. Place the eggs and sugar in a bowl over hot water. (If using an electric whisk the hot water is unnecessary.) Whisk for about 10 minutes until the mixture is light and thick and leaves a trail from the whisk.
3. Sift the flour, cocoa and coffee into the bowl and fold in lightly using a metal spoon.
4. Divide the mixture between the prepared tins. Shake the tins to level the mixture.
5. Bake in a preheated oven for 20–25 minutes, until the cakes are firm to the touch. Turn out and cool on a wire tray.
6. To make the icing, break up the chocolate and place in a bowl over a pan of hot water until melted.
7. Place the egg whites and icing sugar in a bowl over a pan of hot water. Whisk with an electric whisk until light and thick and the mixture stands in peaks. Remove from the heat and whisk for 2 minutes.
8. Whisk the butter until creamy, gradually whisk in the meringue, then whisk in the chocolate.
9. To make the praline, spread a piece of foil over a board and brush it with oil. Place the sugar and almonds in a heavy-based saucepan. Heat gently until the sugar has melted and turned golden brown.
10. Pour the praline over the foil and leave until hard, then place between 2 sheets of greaseproof paper and crush with a rolling pin.
11. Slice each cake in half. Spread each layer with some of the icing and assemble on a serving plate.
12. Spread some more icing over the top and sides of the cake. Press the crushed praline on to the sides.
13. Place the remaining icing in a piping bag fitted with a star tube. Pipe rosettes around the top edge of the cake. Place a few chocolate curls in the centre.

STRAWBERRY CREAM GÂTEAU

Makes one 20 cm (8 inch) cake
3 eggs
75 g (3 oz) caster sugar
75 g (3 oz) plain flour
25 g (1 oz) butter, melted
Filling and decoration:
300 ml (½ pint) double or whipping cream
350 g (12 oz) strawberries
2 tablespoons redcurrant jelly

Preparation time: 20 minutes
Cooking time: 20–25 minutes
Oven: 180°C, 350°F, Gas Mark 4

1. Grease and line two 20 cm (8 inch) sandwich tins.
2. Place the eggs and sugar in a bowl over hot water. (If using an electric whisk the hot water is unnecessary.) Whisk for about 10 minutes until the mixture is light and thick and leaves a trail when the whisk is lifted from it.
3. Sift the flour into the bowl and fold in lightly, using a metal spoon, until evenly mixed. Pour the melted butter slowly into the mixture and fold in.
4. Pour the mixture into the prepared tins. Shake the tins to level the mixture. Bake in a preheated oven for 20–25 minutes until the cake is golden brown and firm to the touch.
5. Turn out and cool on a wire tray.
6. Whip the cream until stiff, then slice half the strawberries.
7. Spread one third of the cream over 1 cake and cover with the sliced strawberries.
8. Spread half the remaining cream over the top of the cake. Cut the remaining strawberries in half and place on the top of the cake to within 3 cm (1 inch) of the edge.
9. Warm the redcurrant jelly and brush over the strawberries.
10. Place the remaining cream in a piping bag fitted with a star tube. Pipe rosettes around the top edge of the cake.

Variation:
When strawberries are not available or too expensive, try this gâteau with any other colourful fruit in season. Blackberries, peach slices, dessert plums, halved, or kiwi fruit are all suitable. To glaze the lighter coloured fruits, replace the redcurrant jelly with warmed, sieved apricot jam.

Mocha praline gâteau; Strawberry cream gâteau

YOGURT AND HONEY CAKE

Makes 24 bars

4 eggs, separated
225 g (8 oz) caster sugar
100 g (4 oz) butter, melted
200 ml (⅓ pint) plain unsweetened yogurt
¼ teaspoon bicarbonate of soda
275 g (10 oz) plain flour
3 teaspoons baking powder
100 g (4 oz) clear honey
4 tablespoons water
strip of lemon rind
cinnamon stick
50 g (2 oz) flaked almonds, toasted

Preparation time: 15 minutes
Cooking time: 25 minutes
Oven: 190°C, 375°F, Gas Mark 5

1. Grease a 33 cm × 23 cm (13 inch × 9 inch) shallow oblong tin.

2. Place the egg yolks and sugar in a bowl and whisk either by hand or using an electric whisk on high speed until light and thick, about 5 minutes.

3. Whisk in the melted butter. Mix together the yogurt and bicarbonate of soda and stir in.

4. Whisk the egg whites until stiff. Fold lightly into the mixture with a metal spoon.

5. Sift the flour and baking powder into the bowl and fold in lightly until well mixed.

6. Pour the mixture into the prepared tin and smooth the top.

7. Bake in a preheated oven for 25 minutes until the cake is golden brown and springs back when pressed with the fingers. Leave to cool in the tin.

8. Place the honey, water, lemon rind and cinnamon stick in a saucepan. Heat gently for 5 minutes.

9. Remove the lemon rind and cinnamon stick and pour the syrup evenly over the cake. Sprinkle with the almonds.

10. Leave until the syrup is cold, then cut the cake into 3 lengthways and 8 across.

CHOCOLATE ROULADE

175 g (6 oz) plain chocolate, broken into pieces
5 eggs, separated
175 g (6 oz) caster sugar
150 ml (¼ pint) double cream

Preparation time: 15 minutes, plus cooling
Cooking time: 20 minutes
Oven: 180°C, 350°F, Gas Mark 4

A moist, mousse-like roll to serve as a dessert.

1. Grease and line a 33 cm × 23 cm (13 inch × 9 inch) Swiss roll tin.
2. Melt the chocolate in a bowl over hot water.
3. Place the egg yolks and sugar in a bowl over hot water. (If using an electric whisk the hot water is unnecessary.) Whisk until the mixture is pale and creamy, about 5 minutes. Whisk in the chocolate.
4. Whisk the egg whites until they form stiff peaks, then fold carefully into the chocolate mixture. Pour into the prepared tin and shake gently to level.
5. Bake in a preheated oven for 20 minutes until firm. Cover with a sheet of foil and leave until completely cold, about 3 hours, then turn out the roulade on to a sheet of greaseproof paper.
6. Whisk the cream until it holds its shape, then spread evenly over the roulade. Roll up from one short end. It will crack quite naturally at this stage.

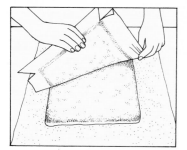

Place a sheet of greaseproof paper on the working surface and sprinkle lightly with caster sugar. Turn out the sponge carefully on to it. Peel away the paper lining the tin.

Trim off each of the edges to make a neat rectangle and spread evenly with either jam or cream.

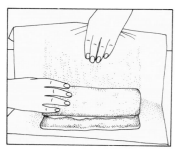

To roll up, turn over the bottom short edge of the sponge. Then, holding the sugared paper in one hand, gradually lift it, while gently rolling the sponge with the other.

SWISS ROLL

3 eggs
75 g (3 oz) caster sugar
75 g (3 oz) plain flour
caster sugar, for sprinkling
3 tablespoons strawberry jam

Preparation time: 15 minutes
Cooking time: 8–10 minutes
Oven: 200°C, 400°F, Gas Mark 6

1. Grease and line a 33 cm × 23 cm (13 inch × 9 inch) Swiss roll tin.
2. Place the eggs and sugar in a bowl over hot water. (If using an electric whisk the hot water is unnecessary.) Whisk for about 10 minutes until the mixture is light and thick and leaves a trail when the whisk is lifted from it.
3. Sift the flour into the bowl and fold in lightly using a metal spoon until evenly mixed.
4. Place the mixture in the prepared tin. Shake the tin to level the mixture.

5. Bake in a preheated oven for 8–10 minutes, until light golden and firm to the touch.
6. Spread a piece of greaseproof paper on a working surface and sprinkle evenly with caster sugar.
7. Turn the cake out on to the paper and remove the paper it was cooked in. Trim off the edges of the cake and spread quickly with the jam.
8. Roll up from one short end using the sugared greaseproof paper to help you. Leave to cool.

Variations:
Chocolate Cream Roll: Replace 15 g (½ oz) of the flour with cocoa. Roll up the Swiss roll without filling, rolling up the greaseproof paper with the cake. When cold, carefully unroll and spread with 150 ml (¼ pint) whipped double cream. Roll up again (without the paper) and chill until served.
Orange Swiss Roll: Add the grated rind of 1 orange to the cake mixture. Beat together 100 g (4 oz) butter, 225 g (8 oz) icing sugar, the grated rind of ½ orange and 3 tablespoons of orange juice. Fill the Swiss roll, once it has been rolled and chilled as for the Chocolate Cream roll, with half the icing and spread the remainder over the top.

GENOESE FANCIES

Makes 25–30
2 eggs
50 g (2 oz) caster sugar
50 g (2 oz) plain flour
25 g (1 oz) butter, melted
Icing and decoration:
1 tablespoon apricot jam, warmed
175 g (6 oz) marzipan
350 g (12 oz) icing sugar
3 tablespoons hot water
assorted nuts, cherries, jelly sweets (see method)
few drops of various food colourings (see method)

Preparation time: 35 minutes
Cooking time: 20–25 minutes
Oven: 180°C, 350°F, Gas Mark 4

1. Grease and bottom-line a 20 cm (8 inch) square cake tin.
2. Place the eggs and sugar in a bowl over hot water. (If using an electric whisk the hot water is unnecessary.) Whisk for about 10 minutes until the mixture is light and thick and leaves a trail when the whisk is lifted from it.
3. Sift the flour in the bowl and fold in lightly using a metal spoon until evenly mixed. Pour the melted butter slowly into the mixture and fold in.
4. Pour the mixture into the prepared tin. Bake in a preheated oven for 20–25 minutes, until golden brown and firm to the touch.
5. Leave in the tin for 5 minutes, then turn out to cool on a wire tray.
6. Place the cake on a board and brush the top with the jam. Roll out three-quarters of the marzipan and cover the top of the cake.
7. Cut the cake into squares, triangles, rounds and diamonds. Shape the remaining marzipan into balls and place on top of each cake.
8. Beat together the icing sugar and hot water until smooth and glossy and the icing will coat the back of a spoon.
9. Place a cake on a palette knife and spoon over the icing to coat. Carefully transfer to a wire tray and decorate with a nut, a piece of cherry or the decoration of your choice.
10. Coat a few more cakes with white icing. Mix a few drops of food colouring with a little icing and use to coat more cakes, using the colourings and toppings of your choice.
11. Leave the cakes until the icing has set.

COCONUT BREAD

Makes one 1.5 kg (3 lb) loaf
150 g (5 oz) desiccated coconut
450 ml (¾ pint) milk
400 g (14 oz) plain flour
2 teaspoons baking powder
¼ teaspoon ground cloves
¼ teaspoon ground cinnamon
½ teaspoon salt
275 g (10 oz) caster sugar

Preparation time: 10 minutes, plus soaking
Cooking time: 1¼–1½ hours
Oven: 180°C, 350°F, Gas Mark 4

This cake from the West Indies is surprisingly moist and rich despite its lack of eggs and fat.

1. Mix together the coconut and milk. Leave to stand for 30 minutes.
2. Sift the flour, baking powder, cloves, cinnamon and salt into a bowl. Stir in the sugar.
3. Mix the coconut milk into the dry ingredients to make a soft batter.
4. Pour the mixture into a greased 1.5 kg (3 lb) loaf tin. Smooth over the top.
5. Bake in a preheated oven for 1¼–1½ hours until light golden and firm to the touch.
6. Turn out and cool on a wire tray. Serve sliced and buttered.

STICKY GINGERBREAD Ⓜ

Makes about 15
275 g (10 oz) plain flour
2 teaspoons ground ginger
1 teaspoon bicarbonate of soda
100 g (4 oz) margarine
100 g (4 oz) soft light brown sugar
225 g (8 oz) golden syrup
100 g (4 oz) black treacle
2 eggs, beaten
150 ml (¼ pint) hot water

Preparation time: 15 minutes
Cooking time: 45 minutes
Oven: 180°C, 350°F, Gas Mark 4

1. Grease and line a 30 cm × 23 cm (12 inch × 9 inch) roasting tin.
2. Sift the flour, ginger and bicarbonate of soda into a large mixing bowl.
3. Place the margarine, sugar, syrup and treacle in a saucepan. Heat gently until the margarine has melted and the sugar has dissolved.
4. Make a well in the centre of the dry ingredients. Pour the mixture from the saucepan into the flour and beat well to mix.
5. Add the beaten eggs and hot water and mix to a smooth batter.
6. Pour the mixture into the prepared tin.
7. Bake in a preheated oven for 45 minutes until the cake springs back when pressed with the fingers.
8. Turn out of the tin, remove the paper and cool on a wire tray. Keep for 2 days before eating, then cut into slices to serve. To store, wrap in greaseproof paper, then foil. It will keep for up to 2 weeks.

Sticky gingerbread; Date and lemon loaf

YORKSHIRE PARKIN

Makes 12
2 teaspoons bicarbonate of soda
150 ml (¼ pint) milk
175 g (6 oz) golden syrup
50 g (2 oz) black treacle
75 g (3 oz) granulated sugar
100 g (4 oz) lard
100 g (4 oz) butter or margarine
225 g (8 oz) porridge oats
225 g (8 oz) plain flour
2 teaspoons ground ginger
½ teaspoon salt

Preparation time: 10 minutes
Cooking time: 1 hour
Oven: 160°C, 325°F, Gas Mark 3

Oatmeal was traditionally used to make parkin but as it is not so widely available now I have substituted porridge oats which works just as well.

1. Grease and line a 20 cm (8 inch) square cake tin.
2. Dissolve the bicarbonate of soda in the milk.
3. Place the syrup, treacle, sugar and fats in a large saucepan. Heat gently until the sugar has dissolved and the fats have melted.
4. Remove from the heat and stir in the oats, flour, ginger, salt and the milk mixture. Mix well together.
5. Pour the mixture into the prepared tin and bake in a preheated oven for 1 hour until deep brown.
6. Leave to cool in the tin, then turn out and remove the paper. Wrap in greaseproof paper, then foil and store for 1–2 days before eating, to bring out the flavour and make it moister.

DATE AND LEMON LOAF

Makes one 1.5 kg (3 lb) loaf
225 g (8 oz) stoneless dates, chopped
175 g (6 oz) margarine
175 g (6 oz) soft dark brown sugar
75 g (3 oz) golden syrup
grated rind of 1 lemon
3 eggs, beaten
275 g (10 oz) self-raising flour
½ teaspoon salt
Topping:
2 tablespoons plain flour
1 tablespoon demerara sugar
15 g (½ oz) butter

Preparation time: 15 minutes
Cooking time: 1 hour 25 minutes
Oven: 160°C, 325°F, Gas Mark 3

1. Grease and bottom-line a 1.5 kg (3 lb) loaf tin.
2. Place the dates, margarine, sugar and syrup in a large saucepan. Heat gently until the margarine has melted and the sugar has dissolved.
3. Remove from the heat, cool slightly, then stir in the lemon rind and beaten eggs. Stir in the flour and salt and mix thoroughly.
4. Place the mixture in the prepared tin.
5. To make the topping, mix together the flour and sugar, then rub in the butter to form a crumble.
6. Sprinkle the crumble evenly over the loaf. Bake in a preheated oven for 1 hour 25 minutes until the cake is golden brown and springs back when pressed with the fingers.
7. Cool the loaf in the tin for 15 minutes, then turn out and leave to cool completely on a wire tray.

BARNSTAPLE GINGERBREADS

Makes 18–20
50 g (2 oz) butter
50 g (2 oz) caster sugar
75 g (3 oz) golden syrup
1 teaspoon lemon juice
50 g (2 oz) plain flour
1 teaspoon ground ginger

Preparation time: 10 minutes, plus cooling
Cooking time: 10–12 minutes per batch
Oven: 180°C, 350°F, Gas Mark 4

These biscuits are similar to brandy snaps but they are made flat instead of being rolled up. They are very good served with ice cream and cold sweets.

1. Place the butter, sugar and syrup in a saucepan. Heat gently until the butter has melted and the sugar has dissolved.
2. Remove from the heat and add the lemon juice, flour and ginger. Mix well, then leave until cold.
3. Grease 3 baking sheets. Place barely level teaspoons of the mixture, with plenty of space between, on the baking sheets. Bake 1 tray at a time in a preheated oven for 10–12 minutes each.
4. When the biscuits are flat and golden brown, remove from the oven and cool for 1 minute.
5. Remove with a palette knife and cool on a wire tray. Cook the remaining biscuits in the same way.

BRAZILIAN CHOCOLATE AND ORANGE CAKE

Makes 16 wedges
350 g (12 oz) plain chocolate
100 g (4 oz) butter
75 g (3 oz) golden syrup
grated rind of 1 orange
100 g (4 oz) sultanas
350 g (12 oz) digestive biscuits, broken up
3 tablespoons dark rum

Preparation time: 15 minutes, plus chilling

1. Grease and bottom-line an 18 cm (7 inch) round loose-based cake tin.
2. Break up the chocolate and place in a saucepan over a low heat with the butter and syrup. Heat gently, stirring, until smooth and glossy, about 5 minutes.
3. Stir in the orange rind, sultanas, biscuits and rum.
4. Pour the mixture into the prepared tin. Leave until cool, then chill until firm.
5. Remove from the tin and cut into small wedges.

PASSION CAKE

Makes one 20 cm (8 inch) cake
150 g (5 oz) butter
200 g (7 oz) soft light brown sugar
175 g (6 oz) grated carrots
½ teaspoon salt
1 teaspoon mixed spice
2 eggs
200 g (7 oz) self-raising flour
2 teaspoons baking powder
100 g (4 oz) walnuts, finely chopped
Icing and decoration:
225 g (8 oz) full fat soft cheese
2–3 tablespoons lemon juice
50 g (2 oz) icing sugar, sifted
25 g (1 oz) walnuts, chopped

Preparation time: 20 minutes
Cooking time: 1 hour
Oven: 180°C, 350°F, Gas Mark 4

1. Grease and line a 20 cm (8 inch) round cake tin.
2. Melt the butter and pour into a mixing bowl. Beat in the sugar, carrots, salt, spice and eggs.
3. Sift the flour and baking powder and add the 100 g (4 oz) walnuts. Fold into the carrot mixture lightly until evenly mixed.
4. Place the mixture in the prepared tin. Bake in a preheated oven for 1 hour, until firm to the touch and golden brown.
5. Cool in the tin for 5 minutes, then turn out and cool completely on a wire tray.
6. Beat the cheese until smooth. Gradually beat in the lemon juice according to taste, then beat in the icing sugar until well mixed.
7. Split the cake in half and spread with one-third of the icing. Spread the remaining icing over the top and sides of the cake, marking with a fork.
8. Sprinkle the top edge of the cake with the chopped walnuts.

Variation:
Bake the cake mixture in paper cake cases to make small passion cakes. The above quantity will make about 24 cakes. Half fill the cases, then bake for 20–25 minutes. When cool spread them with the cream cheese frosting and top each with a walnut half.

Passion cake; Barnstaple gingerbreads

BOILED FRUIT CAKE

Makes one 22 cm (9 inch) cake

175 g (6 oz) raisins
175 g (6 oz) sultanas
150 g (5 oz) currants
300 ml (½ pint) water
100 g (4 oz) butter
150 g (5 oz) soft dark brown sugar
3 eggs, beaten
275 g (10 oz) self-raising flour
2 teaspoons mixed spice
2 tablespoons marmalade
25 g (1 oz) blanched almonds, chopped
100 g (4 oz) glacé cherries, chopped
100 g (4 oz) cut mixed peel
3 tablespoons whisky (optional)
icing sugar, for sprinkling

Preparation time: 15 minutes
Cooking time: 1½ hours
Oven: 180°C, 350°F, Gas Mark 4

1. Grease and bottom-line a 22 cm (9 inch) round cake tin.

2. Place the raisins, sultanas, currants, water, butter and sugar in a large saucepan. Heat gently until the butter has melted, then remove from the heat and cool slightly.

3. Add the beaten eggs, flour, spice, marmalade, almonds, cherries, peel and whisky (if using) to the pan. Mix thoroughly.

4. Pour the mixture into the prepared tin. Bake in a preheated oven for 1½ hours, until the cake is deep golden brown and springs back when pressed with the fingers.

5. Cool the cake in the tin for 30 minutes, then turn out and leave to cool completely on a wire tray.

6. Sprinkle the top of the cake thickly with icing sugar. To store, wrap first in greaseproof paper, then foil and place in an airtight tin. It will keep for about 2 weeks.

MACAROONS

Makes 10
100 g (4 oz) ground almonds
100 g (4 oz) caster sugar
2 egg whites
½ teaspoon almond essence
rice paper, for lining
10 whole almonds

Preparation time: 10 minutes
Cooking time: 20–25 minutes
Oven: 180°C, 350°F, Gas Mark 4

1. Mix together the ground almonds and sugar.
2. Whisk the egg whites until stiff. Fold the almond mixture and essence into the egg whites.
3. Place the mixture in a piping bag fitted with a large plain tube. Pipe 10 rounds about 5 cm (2 inches) across on to a baking sheet lined with rice paper. Press an almond into the centre of each.
4. Bake in a preheated oven for 20–25 minutes, until lightly browned and firm. Remove and cool on a wire tray, then trim off the extra rice paper.

FLORENTINES

Makes 18–20
50 g (2 oz) butter
50 g (2 oz) demerara sugar
1 tablespoon golden syrup
50 g (2 oz) glacé cherries, chopped
25 g (1 oz) shelled walnuts, chopped
25 g (1 oz) sultanas
25 g (1 oz) cut mixed peel
25 g (1 oz) plain flour
50 g (2 oz) flaked almonds
1 teaspoon lemon juice
100 g (4 oz) plain chocolate, melted

Preparation time: 20 minutes
Cooking time: 12–15 minutes
Oven: 190°C, 375°F, Gas Mark 5

1. Place the butter, sugar and syrup in a saucepan. Heat gently until the butter has melted and the sugar has dissolved. Add the remaining ingredients, *except* the chocolate and mix well.
2. Place teaspoonsful of the mixture, well apart, on greased baking sheets. Bake in a preheated oven for 12–15 minutes, until well spread and golden brown.
3. Leave for 1 minute, then transfer to a wire tray using a palette knife and cool completely.
4. Spread the base of each with the melted chocolate, making wavy lines with a fork. Leave to set.

CHORNS

Makes about 25
75 g (3 oz) plain flour
100 g (4 oz) caster sugar
50 g (2 oz) desiccated coconut
50 g (2 oz) porridge oats
25 g (1 oz) walnuts, chopped
1 teaspoon bicarbonate of soda
2 tablespoons golden syrup
100 g (4 oz) butter
3 tablespoons water

Preparation time: 10 minutes
Cooking time: 12–15 minutes
Oven: 180°C, 350°F, Gas Mark 4

1. Mix together the flour, sugar, coconut, oats, walnuts and bicarbonate of soda in a bowl.
2. Place the syrup and butter in a saucepan. Heat gently until the butter has melted. Add the dry ingredients and the water to the saucepan and mix well.
3. Shape the mixture into balls about 2.5 cm (1 inch) across. Place a little apart, on greased baking sheets.
4. Bake in a preheated oven for 12–15 minutes, until golden brown.
5. Leave on the baking sheets for 2 minutes, then transfer to a wire tray to cool completely.

MUESLI BARS

Makes 18
3 tablespoons honey
100 g (4 oz) butter
50 g (2 oz) soft light brown sugar
50 g (2 oz) chopped mixed nuts
100 g (4 oz) porridge oats
25 g (1 oz) desiccated coconut
50 g (2 oz) sesame seeds
100 g (4 oz) plain chocolate, melted (optional)

Preparation time: 10 minutes
Cooking time: 20 minutes
Oven: 180°C, 350°F, Gas Mark 4

1. Place the honey, butter and sugar in a saucepan. Heat gently until the butter has melted and the sugar has dissolved.
2. Stir in the nuts, oats, coconut and sesame seeds.
3. Press evenly into a greased 28 cm × 18 cm (11 inch × 7 inch) shallow oblong tin. Bake in a preheated oven for 20 minutes, until golden brown.
4. Cool for 5 minutes in the tin, then cut into 3 lengthways and 6 across. Leave in the tin to cool completely. Dip one end of the bar in the melted chocolate, if using.

YEASTED BAKES

HARVEST WHEATSHEAF

225 g (8 oz) White bread dough (page 54)
beaten egg, to glaze
2 currants

Preparation time: 45 minutes, plus rising
Cooking time: 35 minutes
Oven: 200°C, 400°F, Gas Mark 6

This beautiful loaf is easier to make than it looks. If you would like to keep it, return the cooked wheatsheaf to a cool oven and dry it out for a couple of hours.

1. Make the dough according to the master recipe for White bread on page 54, up to and including step 7, then divide the dough into 4 equal pieces.
2. Roll out a quarter of the dough to a basic wheatsheaf shape, about 25 cm (10 inches) across the top and 20 cm (8 inches) across the base. Place on a large greased baking sheet and brush with some of the beaten egg.
3. Divide a second piece of dough into 4, then each of these into 6, to make 24 small pieces.
4. Roll each piece to a sausage 15 cm (6 inches) long. Place below the waist of the wheatsheaf to form stalks. Brush with egg as you go. Twist 2 strips together to form the tie across the waist.
5. Shape another small piece into a field mouse among stalks, using currants for the eyes.
6. Roll out the remaining two pieces of dough to form 1 oblong 40 cm × 20 cm (16 inches × 8 inches). Cut into 2.5 cm (1 inch) wide strips, then cut each strip into diamond shapes.
7. Snip each diamond shape several times with scissors to form wheat ears.
8. Place the ears over the top of the wheatsheaf starting around the edge and overlapping them. Brush the ears with egg as you go.
9. Cover the wheatsheaf with oiled polythene and leave to rise for 20 minutes.
10. Brush again with egg and bake in a preheated oven for 35 minutes until golden brown.

SHORT-TIME WHITE BREAD

Makes 3 large loaves
50 g (2 oz) fresh yeast
900 ml (1½ pints) warm water
50 mg tablet vitamin C, crushed
1½ kg (3 lb) white bread flour
4 teaspoons salt
1 tablespoon sugar
50 g (2 oz) butter, margarine or lard
flour, for sprinkling

Preparation time: 20 minutes, plus rising
Cooking time: 30–35 minutes
Oven: 230°C, 450°F, Gas Mark 8

I have found that fresh yeast works best for this recipe, as, when used with a small amount of Vitamin C, it speeds up the rising.

1. Blend the yeast with 300 ml (½ pint) of the water. Add the crushed vitamin C tablet.
2. Mix together the flour, salt and sugar in a large mixing bowl and rub in the fat.
3. Add the yeast liquid and remaining water and mix to a soft dough.
4. Turn the dough out on to a floured surface and knead for about 10 minutes, until it is smooth and silky and no longer sticky.
5. Divide the dough into 3 equal pieces. Shape each piece into an oblong and place into greased 1 kg (2 lb) loaf tins.
6. Cover loosely with oiled polythene and leave to rise for about 1 hour, until doubled in size.
7. Sprinkle the loaves with flour and bake in a preheated oven for 30–35 minutes, until deep golden brown and the bread sounds hollow when tapped at the base. Remove from the tins and cool on a wire tray.

WHITE BREAD M

Makes 3 large loaves
900 ml (1½ pints) warm water
2 teaspoons sugar
1 tablespoon dried yeast
1½ kg (3 lb) white bread flour
4 teaspoons salt
50 g (2 oz) butter, margarine or lard
flour, for sprinkling

Preparation time: 30 minutes, plus rising
Oven: 230°C, 450°F, Gas Mark 8

When using dried yeast the temperature of the water you dissolve it in is important. Mix one part boiling water to two parts cold for the correct temperature.

1. Measure 300 ml (½ pint) of the warm water into a jug. Sprinkle over the sugar and yeast. Leave for about 10 minutes, until frothy.
2. Place the flour and salt in a large mixing bowl and rub in the fat.
3. Pour in the yeast liquid and remaining water and mix to a soft dough.
4. Place on a floured surface and knead by folding the dough in half towards you, then pushing it down and away from you. Give it a quarter turn and repeat the action, until you develop a rocking rhythm.
5. Continue kneading for about 10 minutes, until it is smooth and silky and is no longer sticky.
6. Place the dough in a large, oiled polythene bag or bin liner and loosely close the end. Leave the dough until it has doubled in size and will spring back when pressed with a floured finger. This will take 1–1½ hours at room temperature.
7. Remove from the bag and punch the dough to deflate it and knock out the air bubbles. Knead for 2 minutes until firm.
8. Divide the dough into 3 and shape each piece to fit greased 1 kg (2 lb) loaf tins. Place in the tins, sprinkle with flour and cover with oiled polythene.
9. Leave for 30–40 minutes until doubled in size.
10. Bake in a preheated oven for 45 minutes, until deep golden and the bread sounds hollow when tapped at the base. Remove from the tins and cool on a wire tray.

Variations:
Farmhouse loaves: Place the dough in the tins. Just before baking, brush with beaten egg and make a slit with a sharp knife along the length of each loaf.
Bloomer loaves: Shape the dough into 3 sausage shapes about 23 cm (9 inches) long. Place on greased baking sheets and make 6 diagonal slashes 2.5 cm (1 inch) apart across the top of each loaf. Brush with beaten egg, prove and bake as above.

Fold the dough in half towards you.

Push the dough down and away.

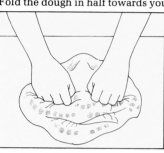

Punch to deflate.

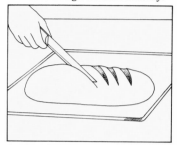

Diagonal slashes for a bloomer loaf.

POPPY SEED PLAIT

Makes 1
300 ml (½ pint) warm water
1 teaspoon sugar
1 teaspoon dried yeast
450 g (1 lb) white bread flour
1½ teaspoons salt
15 g (½ oz) butter, margarine or lard
beaten egg, to glaze
poppy seeds, for sprinkling

Preparation time: 20 minutes, plus rising
Cooking time: 35-40 minutes
Oven: 230°C, 450°F, Gas Mark 8

1. Make up the dough following the recipe for White bread on page 54 up to and including step 5. Place in an oiled polythene bag and leave to rise for about 1 hour, until doubled in size and the dough springs back when pressed.
2. Place on a floured surface and punch with the fists. Knead for 2 minutes until smooth.
3. Divide the dough into 3 equal pieces. Roll each piece into a sausage shape 40 cm (16 inches) long.
4. Join the rolls at one end and plait loosely. Pinch the ends together to seal. Place on a greased baking sheet and cover with oiled polythene. Leave to rise until doubled in size, about 45 minutes.
5. Brush the plait with the beaten egg and sprinkle with poppy seeds. Bake in a preheated oven for 35–40 minutes until deep golden brown and the bread sounds hollow when tapped on the base. Cool on a wire tray.

QUICK WHEATMEAL BREAD

Makes 1
300 ml (½ pint) warm water
2 teaspoons sugar
2 teaspoons dried yeast
450 g (1 lb) wheatmeal flour
1½ teaspoons salt
15 g (½ oz) butter, margarine or lard
cracked wheat or oats, for sprinkling

Preparation time: 10 minutes, plus rising
Cooking time: 30 minutes
Oven: 230°C, 450°F, Gas Mark 8

This loaf can be made and on the table in just over an hour. It is very simply made with just one rising.

1. Measure the warm water into a jug. Sprinkle over 1 teaspoon of the sugar and the yeast and leave for about 10 minutes, until frothy.
2. Place the flour, salt and remaining sugar in a mixing bowl and rub in the fat.
3. Pour the yeast liquid, all at once, into the flour and mix to a soft dough.
4. Place the dough on a floured surface and knead for 5 minutes, until smooth and no longer sticky.
5. Shape the dough into a round and place on a greased baking sheet. Cut a deep cross in the top with a sharp knife.
6. Cover with oiled polythene and leave until doubled in size, about 30 minutes.
7. Remove the polythene and brush with water. Sprinkle with the cracked wheat or oats.
8. Bake in a preheated oven for 30 minutes until brown and crisp and the bread sounds hollow when tapped on the base. Cool on a wire tray.

Variations:
Flowerpot loaf: Clean a flowerpot and dry thoroughly. Smear inside and out with lard and bake in a hot oven for 5 minutes. Repeat this process several times. Grease well before use. Half fill the pots with dough, leave to rise and bake as above.
Tin loaf: Shape the dough into an oblong and place in a greased 1 kg (2 lb) loaf tin. Leave to rise and bake as above.
Rolls: Divide the dough into 12 equal pieces. Shape into balls and place apart on a greased baking sheet. Leave to rise as above and bake for 12–15 minutes at the same temperature as above.

FROM THE TOP: Poppy seed plait; Bloomer loaf;
Quick wheatmeal bread

VIENNA ROLLS

Makes 16
300 ml (½ pint) warm milk and water mixed half and half
1 teaspoon sugar
2 teaspoons dried yeast
450 g (1 lb) white bread flour
1½ teaspoons salt
50 g (2 oz) butter or margarine
beaten egg, to glaze
poppy seeds, for sprinkling

Preparation time: 30 minutes, plus rising
Cooking time: 10–12 minutes
Oven: 220°C, 425°F, Gas Mark 7

1. Measure the liquid into a jug. Sprinkle over the sugar and yeast and leave until frothy, about 10 minutes.
2. Mix the flour and salt in a bowl and rub in the fat. Add the yeast liquid and mix to a soft dough.
3. Place on a floured surface. Knead until smooth, silky and no longer sticky, about 10 minutes.
4. Place the dough in an oiled polythene bag and leave for about 1 hour, until doubled in size and the dough springs back when pressed.
5. Place the dough on a floured surface and punch with the fists. Knead for 2 minutes.
6. Divide into 16 equal pieces. Shape in the following ways and place on greased baking sheets.
Cottage: Pull off one third of the dough and shape both pieces into balls. Place the small ball on top of the larger one and push a floured finger through the centre, right to the bottom.
Clover leaf: Divide the dough into 3. Shape each piece into a ball and place close together on a baking sheet in a triangle.
Figure 8: Shape the dough into a 15 cm (6 inch) long sausage. Curl up from each end to the centre into a figure 8 shape.
Plait: Divide the dough into 3. Shape each piece into a sausage and press the ends together. Plait loosely and pinch the ends to seal.
Knot: Shape the dough into a 15 cm (6 inch) long sausage. Tie in a knot.
Bloomer: Shape the dough into an oval. Make 3 diagonal slashes on the top.
Catherine wheel: Shape the dough into a 15 cm (6 inch) long sausage. Coil up the dough and pinch the end to seal.
7. Brush the rolls with the beaten egg and sprinkle some of the rolls with poppy seeds.
8. Cover with oiled polythene and leave to rise until doubled in size, about 30 minutes.
9. Bake in a preheated oven for 10–12 minutes, until golden brown and the rolls sound hollow when tapped on the base. Cool on a wire tray.

CURRANT BREAD

Makes 1 large loaf
300 ml (½ pint) warm milk
1 teaspoon sugar
2 teaspoons dried yeast
450 g (1 lb) white bread flour
1 teaspoon salt
25 g (1 oz) caster sugar
25 g (1 oz) butter
100 g (4 oz) currants
clear honey, to glaze

Preparation time: 25 minutes, plus rising
Cooking time: 35–40 minutes
Oven: 200°C, 400°F, Gas Mark 6

1. Measure the milk into a jug. Sprinkle over the sugar and yeast and leave until frothy, about 10 minutes.
2. Mix the flour, salt and sugar in a bowl and rub in the butter.
3. Add the yeast liquid and mix to a soft dough.
4. Place on a floured surface. Knead until smooth, silky and no longer sticky, about 10 minutes.
5. Place in an oiled polythene bag and leave until doubled in size, about 1 hour.
6. Place on a floured surface and beat the dough with the fists to remove the air bubbles. Knead the currants into the dough.
7. Shape into an oblong and place in a greased 1 kg (2 lb) loaf tin. Cover with oiled polythene and leave until doubled in size, about 40 minutes.
8. Bake in a preheated oven for 35–40 minutes, until deep golden brown and the bread sounds hollow when tapped on the base.
9. Cool on a wire tray. Brush with honey while still warm. Serve sliced and buttered.

GRANARY TWIST

Makes 2
450 ml (¾ pint) warm water
1 teaspoon sugar
2 teaspoons dried yeast
750 g (1½ lb) granary flour
2 teaspoons salt
25 g (1 oz) butter, margarine or lard
granary flour, for sprinkling

Preparation time: 25 minutes, plus rising
Cooking time: 30–35 minutes
Oven: 230°C, 450°F, Gas Mark 8

1. Measure the water into a jug. Sprinkle over the sugar and yeast and leave until frothy, about 10 minutes.
2. Place the flour and salt in a mixing bowl and rub in the fat.
3. Add the yeast liquid and mix to a soft dough.
4. Place the dough on a floured surface and knead until no longer sticky, about 5 minutes.
5. Place in a large oiled polythene bag or bin liner and leave until doubled in size, about 1 hour.
6. Turn out on a floured surface and punch the dough with the fists, then knead again for 2 minutes.
7. Divide the dough in half. Divide each piece in half again and shape into 4 sausages 30 cm (12 inches) long.
8. Twist 2 of the sausages together and place on a greased baking sheet. Repeat with the other two.
9. Sprinkle with granary flour and cover with oiled polythene. Leave to rise for 30–40 minutes, until doubled in size.
10. Bake in a preheated oven for 30–35 minutes until the bread sounds hollow when tapped on the base. Cool on a wire tray.

CHEESE AND HERB BREAD

Makes 1 large loaf
25 g (1 oz) butter
1 small onion, chopped
300 ml (½ pint) warm water
1 teaspoon sugar
2 teaspoons dried yeast
450 g (1 lb) wheatmeal flour
1½ teaspoons salt
1 teaspoon dry mustard
2 teaspoons mixed dried herbs *or* 1 tablespoon freshly
   chopped herbs
125 g (5 oz) Cheddar cheese, finely grated

Preparation time: 20 minutes, plus rising
Cooking time: 35–40 minutes
Oven: 230°C, 450°F, Gas Mark 8

1. Melt the butter in a small pan, add the onion and fry until softened, about 5 minutes.
2. Measure the water into a jug. Sprinkle over the sugar and yeast. Leave until frothy, about 10 minutes.
3. Place the flour, salt, mustard, herbs and 100 g (4 oz) of the cheese in a mixing bowl. Add the onions and mix well.
4. Add the yeast liquid and mix to a soft dough.
5. Place on a floured surface and knead for about 5 minutes.
6. Shape into an oblong and place in a greased 1 kg (2 lb) loaf tin.
7. Cover with oiled polythene and leave to rise until doubled in size, about 35 minutes.
8. Sprinkle the remaining cheese over the top. Bake in a preheated oven for 35–40 minutes, until golden brown and the bread sounds hollow when tapped on the base. Serve warm with butter.

COTTAGE MILK LOAF

Makes 1 large loaf
450 ml (¾ pint) warm milk
1 teaspoon sugar
2 teaspoons dried yeast
750 g (1½lb) white bread flour
2 teaspoons salt
25 g (1 oz) caster sugar
75 g (3 oz) butter or margarine
beaten egg or milk, to glaze

Preparation time: 25 minutes, plus rising
Cooking time: 35–40 minutes
Oven: 230°C, 450°F, Gas Mark 8

1. Place the milk in a bowl. Sprinkle over the sugar and yeast. Leave until frothy, about 10 minutes.
2. Place the flour, salt and sugar in a bowl and rub in the butter or margarine.
3. Add the yeast liquid and mix to a soft dough. Place on a lightly floured surface and knead until silky and no longer sticky, about 10 minutes.
4. Place in an oiled polythene bag and leave until doubled in size and the dough springs back when pressed, about 1 hour. Turn out on a floured surface and punch with the fists. Knead for 2 minutes.
5. Remove one-third of the dough. Shape the larger piece into a round and place on a greased baking sheet. Then shape the small piece into a round and place on top. Press a floured wooden spoon handle through the centre of the dough, to the bottom.
6. Cover with oiled polythene and leave to rise until doubled in size, about 45 minutes.
7. Brush with the beaten egg or milk and bake in a preheated oven for 35–40 minutes until deep golden brown and the bread sounds hollow when tapped on the base. Cool on a wire tray.

BATCH ROLLS

Makes 12
300 ml (½ pint) warm water
1 teaspoon sugar
1 teaspoon dried yeast
450 g (1 lb) white bread flour
1½ teaspoons salt
15 g (½ oz) butter, margarine or lard
flour, for sprinkling

Preparation time: 20 minutes, plus rising
Cooking time: 20 minutes
Oven: 230°C, 450°F, Gas Mark 8

1. Make up the dough following the recipe for White bread on page 54 up to and including step 5. Place in an oiled polythene bag and leave to rise for about 1 hour, until doubled in size and the dough springs back when pressed.
2. Place on a floured surface and punch with the fists. Knead for 2 minutes until smooth.
3. Divide the dough into 12 equal pieces. Shape into rounds and place them close together on a greased baking sheet in an oblong arrangement.
4. Cover the rolls with oiled polythene and leave until doubled in size, about 30 minutes.
5. Dust with flour and bake in a preheated oven for 20 minutes, until golden brown.
6. Cool on a wire tray and pull rolls apart to serve.

Apple and cinnamon doughnuts

SESAME BAPS

Makes 8

300 ml (½ pint) warm water
1 teaspoon sugar
1 teaspoon dried yeast
450 g (1 lb) white bread flour
1½ teaspoons salt
15 g (½ oz) butter, margarine or lard
sesame seeds, toasted, for sprinkling
flour, for dredging

Preparation time: 30 minutes, plus rising
Cooking time: 15 minutes
Oven: 230°C, 450°F, Gas Mark 8

1. Make up the dough following the recipe for White bread on page 54 up to and including step 7.
2. Divide the dough into 8 equal pieces. Shape each piece into a ball, then flatten with the hand until it is 1 cm (½ inch) thick. Place apart on greased baking sheets.
3. Cover with oiled polythene and leave to rise until doubled in size, about 35 minutes.
4. Brush the baps with water and sprinkle with sesame seeds, then dredge with flour.
5. Bake in a preheated oven for 15 minutes until the baps are golden brown and sound hollow when tapped on the base. Cool on a wire tray.

APPLE AND CINNAMON DOUGHNUTS

Makes 12

85 ml (3 fl oz) warm milk
½ teaspoon sugar
2 teaspoons dried yeast
225 g (8 oz) white bread flour
½ teaspoon salt
75 g (3 oz) caster sugar
25 g (1 oz) butter
1 egg, beaten
100 g (4 oz) apple purée
oil, for deep frying
2 teaspoons ground cinnamon

Preparation time: 25 minutes, plus rising
Cooking time: about 12 minutes

1. Place the milk in a bowl. Sprinkle over the sugar and yeast and leave for 5 minutes. Beat in 50 g (2 oz) of the flour and leave until frothy, about 20 minutes.
2. Place the remaining flour, salt and 25 g (1 oz) of the caster sugar in a bowl. Rub in the butter.
3. Add the flour mixture and beaten egg to the yeast batter and mix to a soft dough.
4. Place on a floured surface. Knead until smooth, silky and no longer sticky, about 10 minutes.
5. Place in an oiled polythene bag and leave until doubled in size, about 1 hour.
6. Turn out on to a floured surface and punch with the fists to remove the air, then knead for 2 minutes.
7. Divide into 12 equal pieces. Roll out to 10 cm (4 inch) rounds. Place a teaspoonful of apple purée in the centre and draw up the dough around it, pinching the edges to seal. Place on a greased baking sheet. Cover with oiled polythene and leave to rise until doubled in size, about 40 minutes.
8. Heat the oil in a deep saucepan to 180°C, 350°F. Fry the doughnuts, until puffy and golden brown.
9. Drain on kitchen paper. Mix the cinnamon with the remaining caster sugar and toss the doughnuts.

ALMOND WHIRL LOAF

Serves 8–10
85 ml (3 fl oz) warm milk
½ teaspoon sugar
2 teaspoons dried yeast
225 g (8 oz) white bread flour
½ teaspoon salt
25 g (1 oz) caster sugar
25 g (1 oz) butter
1 egg, beaten
Filling and decoration:
100 g (4 oz) ground almonds
50 g (2 oz) caster sugar
1 egg white, beaten
½ teaspoon almond essence
75 g (3 oz) glacé cherries, chopped
25 g (1 oz) raisins
100 g (4 oz) icing sugar, sifted
1 tablespoon warm water
1 tablespoon toasted flaked almonds

Preparation time: 25 minutes, plus rising
Cooking time: 35–40 minutes
Oven: 200°C, 400°F, Gas Mark 6

1. Place the milk in a mixing bowl. Sprinkle over the sugar and yeast and leave for 5 minutes, until just beginning to froth.
2. Beat in 50 g (2 oz) of the flour and leave for 20 minutes until frothy.
3. Place the remaining flour, the salt and caster sugar in a bowl, then rub in the butter.
4. Add the yeast liquid and beaten egg to the flour mixture and mix to a soft dough.
5. Place on a floured surface. Knead until smooth, silky and no longer sticky, about 10 minutes.
6. Place in an oiled polythene bag and leave to rise until doubled in size, about 1 hour.
7. Turn out on to a floured surface and punch the dough with the fists, then knead for 2 minutes. Grease a 1 kg (2 lb) loaf tin.
8. Mix the almonds, caster sugar, beaten egg white and almond essence to a paste.
9. Roll out the dough to an oblong 30 cm (12 inches) long by the length of tin. Spread with the almond paste and sprinkle with 50 g (2 oz) of the cherries and all the raisins.
10. Roll up the dough from one short end and place in the prepared tin. Cover and leave to rise until doubled in size, about 1 hour.
11. Bake in a preheated oven for 35–40 minutes, until golden brown and firm. Cool on a wire tray.
12. Beat together the icing sugar and water until smooth and glossy. Drizzle over the loaf and sprinkle with the remaining cherries, together with the toasted almonds.

CHELSEA BUNS

Makes 9
85 ml (3 fl oz) warm milk
½ teaspoon sugar
2 teaspoons dried yeast
225 g (8 oz) white bread flour
½ teaspoon salt
25 g (1 oz) caster sugar
25 g (1 oz) butter or margarine
1 egg, beaten
Filling:
100 g (4 oz) mixed dried fruit
50 g (2 oz) soft dark brown sugar
15 g (½ oz) butter, melted
clear honey, to glaze

Preparation time: 35 minutes, plus rising
Cooking time: 20–25 minutes
Oven: 220°C, 425°F, Gas Mark 7

1. Place the warm milk in a mixing bowl. Sprinkle over the sugar and yeast and leave for 5 minutes, until it is just beginning to froth.
2. Beat in 50 g (2 oz) of the flour and leave for 20 minutes, until frothy.
3. Mix together the remaining flour, the salt and sugar. Rub in the butter or margarine.
4. Add the flour mixture together with the beaten egg to the yeast batter and mix to a soft dough.
5. Turn out the dough on to a floured surface and knead for about 10 minutes, until smooth, silky and no longer sticky.
6. Place the dough in an oiled polythene bag and leave until doubled in size, about 1 hour.
7. Turn out on to a floured surface and punch the dough with the fists, then knead again for 2 minutes.
8. Mix together the dried fruits and soft brown sugar.
9. Roll out the dough to an oblong 30 cm × 23 cm (12 inches × 9 inches). Brush with the melted butter and sprinkle with the fruit mixture.
10. Roll up the dough from one long side. Cut into 9 equal slices.
11. Place the buns close together in a greased 18 cm (7 inch) cake tin.
12. Cover with oiled polythene and leave until doubled in size, about 40 minutes.
13. Bake in a preheated oven for 20–25 minutes until golden brown. Turn out and cool on a wire tray. Brush with honey while still warm.

Bath buns; Almond whirl loaf

BATH BUNS

Makes 12
125 ml (4 fl oz) warm milk
1 teaspoon sugar
2 teaspoons dried yeast
225 g (8 oz) white bread flour
½ teaspoon salt
25 g (1 oz) butter or margarine
25 g (1 oz) caster sugar
75 g (3 oz) sultanas
25 g (1 oz) cut mixed peel
1 egg, beaten
beaten egg, to glaze
25 g (1 oz) sugar cubes, roughly crushed

Preparation time: 25 minutes, plus rising
Cooking time: 10–15 minutes
Oven: 220°C, 425°F, Gas Mark 7

1. Place the milk in a mixing bowl and sprinkle over the sugar and dried yeast. Leave for 5 minutes, until starting to froth, then beat in 50 g (2 oz) of the flour.
2. Leave in a warm place until frothy, about 20 minutes.
3. Mix the remaining flour and the salt together in a bowl and rub in the butter or margarine. Stir in the sugar, sultanas and peel.
4. Add the flour mixture and the beaten egg to the yeast batter. Mix to a soft dough. Beat with a wooden spoon for 3 minutes, or in a mixer for one.
5. Cover the bowl with polythene and leave to rise for about 1 hour, until doubled in size.
6. Beat again for 1 minute, then place tablespoonsful, well apart, on to greased baking sheets.
7. Brush the buns with beaten egg and sprinkle with crushed sugar cubes.
8. Cover loosely with oiled polythene and leave to prove for about 30 minutes, until doubled in size.
9. Bake in a preheated oven for 10–15 minutes, until golden brown and firm. Serve warm with butter.

HUNGARIAN CAKE

Serves 6–8
150 ml (¼ pint) warm milk
3 teaspoons sugar
2 teaspoons dried yeast
225 g (8 oz) white bread flour
½ teaspoon salt
50 g (2 oz) caster sugar
1 teaspoon ground cinnamon
25 g (1 oz) walnuts, chopped
25 g (1 oz) raisins, chopped
50 g (2 oz) butter, melted

Preparation time: 25 minutes, plus rising
Cooking time: 40 minutes
Oven: 220°C, 425°F, Gas Mark 7

This cake is delicious served with coffee.

1. Measure the milk into a jug. Sprinkle over 1 teaspoon of the sugar and the yeast. Leave until frothy, about 10 minutes.
2. Place the flour, salt and the remaining 2 teaspoons of sugar in a bowl. Mix well.
3. Add the yeast liquid and mix to a soft dough.
4. Place the dough on a floured surface and knead until smooth, silky and no longer sticky, about 10 minutes.
5. Place the dough in an oiled polythene bag and leave until doubled in size and the dough springs back when pressed, about 1 hour.
6. Turn out on to a floured surface and beat with the fists to remove the air bubbles. Knead for 2 minutes.
7. Mix the caster sugar, cinnamon, walnuts and raisins on a plate.
8. Shape the dough into about 14 small balls, 4 cm (1½ inches) across. Coat each ball in the melted butter, then in the mixture on the plate.
9. Place the balls a little apart in 2 layers in a greased 18 cm (7 inch) cake tin. Add any remaining butter and mixture to the tin.
10. Cover and leave to rise until doubled in size, about 45 minutes.
11. Bake in a preheated oven for 40 minutes, until browned and firm to the touch. Turn out and cool on a wire tray.

> Yeast dough rises most quickly in a warm atmosphere but, contrary to popular belief, the best dough is formed in a cool place, so that it rises slowly and produces a strong dough, which will give a light result. The dough will take several hours to rise in the refrigerator and should be brought to room temperature before baking.

PANETTONE

Serves 8–10
1 teaspoon sugar
1 tablespoon dried yeast
4 tablespoons warm milk
100 g (4 oz) butter
50 g (2 oz) caster sugar
3 eggs, beaten
grated rind of ½ lemon
400 g (14 oz) white bread flour
1 teaspoon salt
100 g (4 oz) raisins
75 g (3 oz) cut mixed peel
beaten egg, to glaze

Preparation time: 30 minutes, plus rising
Cooking time: 40 minutes
Oven: 200°C, 400°F, Gas Mark 6;
      180°C, 350°F, Gas Mark 4

This is a traditional fruity bread, eaten at Christmas in Italy.

1. Sprinkle the sugar and yeast over the warm milk in a small bowl. Leave until frothy, about 10 minutes.
2. Beat together the butter and caster sugar until light and fluffy, about 5 minutes. Beat in the eggs, a little at a time, then beat in the lemon rind.
3. Place the flour and salt in a large bowl. Stir in the yeast liquid and creamed mixture and mix until a soft dough is formed.
4. Place the dough on a floured surface and knead until smooth, silky and no longer sticky, about 5 minutes.
5. Place in an oiled polythene bag and leave to rise until doubled in size, about 1 hour.
6. Sprinkle the raisins and peel over the dough and knead until thoroughly and evenly mixed in.
7. Place in a greased 20 cm (8 inch) cake tin and leave until doubled in size, about 45 minutes.
8. Brush the dough with the beaten egg and bake in a preheated oven for 10 minutes, then reduce the oven temperature and bake for a further 30 minutes until deep golden brown and firm to the touch.
9. Serve cut into thin slices and lightly buttered.

> Panettone is a rich yeasted cake which will keep well for up to a week. Wrap it in foil and store it in a container, not an airtight one. Should it become a little dry it is delicious toasted and buttered for tea.

Panettone; Hungarian cake

MALTED TEA BREAD

Makes 2
300 ml (½ pint) warm water
1 teaspoon sugar
1 tablespoon dried yeast
450 g (1 lb) plain flour
1 teaspoon salt
75 g (3 oz) malt extract
50 g (2 oz) black treacle
25 g (1 oz) butter or margarine
225 g (8 oz) sultanas
clear honey, to glaze

Preparation time: 15 minutes, plus rising
Cooking time: 45 minutes
Oven: 200°C, 400°F, Gas Mark 6

1. Measure the water into a jug. Sprinkle over the sugar and yeast and leave for about 10 minutes until frothy.
2. Place the flour and salt in a mixing bowl. Place the malt extract, treacle and butter or margarine in a pan and heat gently until the fat has melted.
3. Make a well in the centre of the flour and pour in the warmed malt mixture, the yeast liquid and the sultanas. Beat well to form a smooth batter.
4. Divide the mixture between 2 greased 450 g (1 lb) loaf tins and place in a large oiled polythene bag. Leave to rise for about 1 hour until the mixture is almost to the top of the tins.
5. Bake in a preheated oven for 45 minutes until firm to the touch.
6. Turn out and cool on a wire tray. Brush with honey while still warm.

DANISH PASTRIES

Makes 16
225 g (8 oz) plain flour
pinch of salt
25 g (1 oz) caster sugar
175 g (6 oz) butter, softened
85 ml (3 fl oz) warm milk
½ teaspoon sugar
2 teaspoons dried yeast
1 egg, beaten
Spice filling:
25 g (1 oz) butter
25 g (1 oz) icing sugar, sifted
1 teaspoon ground cinnamon
25 g (1 oz) currants
Almond filling:
25 g (1 oz) ground almonds
25 g (1 oz) caster sugar
½ egg white
almond essence
To finish:
beaten egg, to glaze
100 g (4 oz) icing sugar, softened
1 tablespoon warm water

Preparation time: about 1 hour, plus chilling and rising
Cooking time: 15 minutes
Oven: 220°C, 425°F, Gas Mark 7

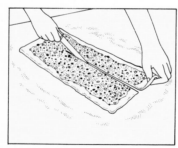
Cutting the spiced dough

Cutting slices

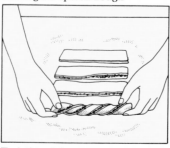
Twisting strips

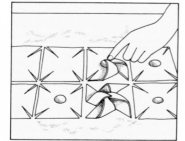
Folding alternate points

1. Place the flour, salt and caster sugar into a bowl. Rub in 25 g (1 oz) of the butter.
2. Measure the warm milk into a jug. Sprinkle over the sugar and yeast and leave for about 10 minutes, until frothy.
3. Place the remaining butter on a flat plate and spread using a round-ended knife to an oblong 20 cm × 10 cm (8 inches × 4 inches). Chill while preparing the dough.
4. Add the yeast liquid and beaten egg to the flour mixture and mix to a soft dough.
5. Place the dough on a floured surface and knead until smooth and elastic, about 5 minutes.
6. Place in an oiled polythene bag and chill for 10 minutes.
7. Roll out the dough to an oblong 38 cm × 13 cm (15 inches × 5 inches). Place the chilled butter in the centre. Fold the bottom third of dough up and top third of dough down to cover it.
8. Seal the edges of the dough and roll out as before. Fold into 3 again and seal the edges. Place in a polythene bag and chill for 10 minutes.
9. Repeat rolling and folding twice more and chill for a further 10 minutes.
10. To make the spice filling, beat together the butter and icing sugar until soft, then beat in the cinnamon and currants.
11. To make the almond filling, beat together the ground almonds, sugar, egg white and a few drops of essence.
12. Roll out half the dough to an oblong 40 cm × 15 cm (16 inches × 6 inches). Spread with the spice filling and cut in half down the length. Roll up one half from one short end and cut into 4 slices. Place on a greased baking sheet.
13. Fold the other half of the dough evenly into 3 and cut into 4 strips. Twist the strips and place on the prepared baking sheet. Brush with some of the beaten egg.
14. Roll out the remaining dough to an oblong 40 cm × 20 cm (16 inches × 8 inches). Cut into 8 squares.
15. Divide the almond filling into 8 and shape into small balls. Place a ball in the centre of each square of dough.
16. Make cuts from each corner of the 4 squares. Bring alternate points into the centre and press to seal. Fold the 2 opposite corners of the remaining 4 pastries to the centre. Brush with the rest of the beaten egg.
17. Cover and leave to rise for 30 minutes.
18. Bake in a preheated oven for about 15 minutes, until golden brown. Cool on a wire tray.
19. Beat together the icing sugar and warm water until smooth and glossy. Drizzle over the pastries.

Danish pastries

SAVARIN

Serves 6

5 tablespoons warm milk
1 teaspoon sugar
2 teaspoons dried yeast
175 g (6 oz) white bread flour
½ teaspoon salt
1 tablespoon caster sugar
3 eggs, beaten
75 g (3 oz) softened butter

To finish:

100 g (4 oz) sugar
300 ml (½ pint) water
3 tablespoons lemon juice
3 tablespoons dark rum
350 g (12 oz) fresh fruit, e.g. strawberries, raspberries,
    plums, bananas, peaches or a mixture
150 ml (¼ pint) double or whipping cream, whipped

Preparation time: 35 minutes, plus rising
Cooking time: 20 minutes
Oven: 200°C, 400°F, Gas Mark 6

1. Place the warm milk in a mixing bowl and sprinkle over the sugar and yeast. Leave for 5 minutes, until just beginning to froth, then beat in 25 g (1 oz) of the flour. Leave for about 20 minutes, until frothy.

2. Mix together the remaining flour, salt and caster sugar. Add this to the yeast batter with the beaten eggs and butter. Beat well with a wooden spoon for 3 minutes.

3. Pour the mixture into a greased 20 cm (8 inch) savarin ring mould. Place loosely in an oiled polythene bag and leave to rise until the mixture is almost to the top of the tin, about 40 minutes.

4. Bake in a preheated oven for 20 minutes until golden brown and firm to the touch.

5. Turn out on to a wire tray and cool while preparing the syrup.

6. To finish, place the sugar and water in a heavy-based saucepan. Heat gently to dissolve the sugar, then increase the heat and boil rapidly for 5 minutes until syrupy. Remove from the heat and stir in the lemon juice and rum.

7. Place the savarin in a deep serving plate and prick all over. Pour over the syrup until it is all absorbed.

8. Fill the centre with fruit and top with cream.

ALL-IN-ONE

DEVIL'S FOOD CAKE

Serves 8–10
50 g (2 oz) cocoa
6 tablespoons boiling water
175 g (6 oz) self-raising flour
2 teaspoons baking powder
175 g (6 oz) caster sugar
175 g (6 oz) soft margarine
4 eggs
Filling and decoration:
450 g (1 lb) icing sugar, sifted
100 g (4 oz) plain chocolate
50 g (2 oz) butter
4 tablespoons milk

Preparation time: 20 minutes
Cooking time: 30–35 minutes
Oven: 180°C, 350°F, Gas Mark 4

1. Grease and bottom-line two 20 cm (8 inch) sandwich tins.
2. Blend the cocoa with the boiling water to make a smooth paste. Place the cocoa paste in a mixing bowl with the flour, baking powder, caster sugar, margarine and eggs.
3. Beat with a wooden spoon until light and fluffy, about 3 minutes (or 1 minute with a mixer). Divide the mixture between the 2 prepared tins and smooth the tops.
4. Bake in a preheated oven for 30–35 minutes, until well risen and firm to the touch. Leave the cake in the tins for 1 minute, then turn out on to a wire tray to cool completely.
5. To make the filling and icing, place the icing sugar, chocolate, butter and milk in a bowl over a saucepan of hot water. Stir the ingredients together until they have melted to a smooth and glossy icing, about 5 minutes.
6. Cool the icing for about 15 minutes, then beat well until thickened, 2–3 minutes. Fill the cake with a little icing, then spread the remaining icing evenly over the top and sides, swirling with a knife.

ORANGE CURD CAKE M

Serves 6–8
100 g (4 oz) self-raising flour
1 teaspoon baking powder
100 g (4 oz) caster sugar
100 g (4 oz) soft margarine
2 eggs
grated rind of 1 orange
Filling and decoration:
2 oranges
25 g (1 oz) caster sugar
100 g (4 oz) curd cheese
caster sugar, for sprinkling

Preparation time: 20–25 minutes
Cooking time: 30 minutes
Oven: 180°C, 350°F, Gas Mark 4

1. Grease and bottom-line two 18 cm (7 inch) sandwich cake tins.
2. Place the flour, baking powder, sugar, margarine, eggs and orange rind in a bowl. Beat with a wooden spoon until light and fluffy, about 3 minutes (or 1 minute with a mixer).
3. Divide the mixture between the 2 prepared cake tins and smooth the tops.
4. Bake in a preheated oven for 30 minutes, until the cakes are golden brown and firm to the touch. Cool in the tins for 1 minute, then turn out and cool on a wire tray.
5. Cut the rind and all the white pith from the oranges, then cut into segments.
6. To make the filling, chop half the orange segments, place in a bowl with the sugar and curd cheese and mix well together.
7. Sandwich the cakes together with the curd cheese filling. Arrange the remaining orange segments on the top and sprinkle with caster sugar.

Orange curd cake; Devil's food cake

TEA BRACK

Makes 2 small loaves
300 ml (½ pint) currants
300 ml (½ pint) sultanas
300 ml (½ pint) soft dark brown sugar
300 ml (½ pint) cold tea
1 egg, beaten
600 ml (1 pint) self-raising flour

Preparation time: 10 minutes, plus overnight soaking
Cooking time: 1¼ hours
Oven: 160°C, 325°F, Gas Mark 3

This cake just couldn't be simpler, use a measuring jug to get the right quantities for the ingredients.

1. Grease and bottom-line two 450 g (1 lb) loaf tins.
2. Place the currants, sultanas, sugar and tea in a bowl. Mix the ingredients together and leave overnight, or for at least 6 hours.
3. Add the beaten egg and flour to the fruit mixture and beat until smooth. Place half the mixture into each tin and smooth the tops.
4. Bake in a preheated oven for 1¼ hours, until firm to the touch. Cool on a wire tray and serve sliced and buttered.

FARMHOUSE FRUIT CAKE

Serves 8–10
225 g (8 oz) self-raising flour
1 teaspoon mixed spice
150 g (5 oz) soft dark brown sugar
150 g (5 oz) margarine
2 eggs
350 g (12 oz) mixed dried fruit
120 ml (4 fl oz) milk
demerara sugar, for sprinkling

Preparation time: 10 minutes
Cooking time: 1¾–2 hours
Oven: 150°C, 300°F, Gas Mark 2

1. Grease and line a 20 cm (8 inch) round cake tin.
2. Place all the cake ingredients in a bowl. Beat together with a wooden spoon until well mixed.
3. Place the mixture in the prepared tin and smooth the top with the back of a spoon.
4. Sprinkle the top of the cake with demerara sugar. Bake in a preheated oven for 1¾–2 hours, until the cake feels firm when pressed.
5. Cool the cake in the tin for 15 minutes, then turn out and allow to cool completely on a wire tray.

CHRISTMAS CANDLE CAKE

Serves 15–20

275 g (10 oz) currants
200 g (7 oz) sultanas
100 g (4 oz) raisins
50 g (2 oz) glacé cherries, halved
50 g (2 oz) blanched almonds, chopped
50 g (2 oz) cut mixed peel
grated rind of 1 lemon
200 g (7 oz) plain flour
1 teaspoon ground mixed spice
½ teaspoon ground nutmeg
½ teaspoon ground cinnamon
50 g (2 oz) ground almonds
150 g (5 oz) softened butter or soft margarine
175 g (6 oz) soft dark brown sugar
4 eggs
2 tablespoons brandy

Icing and decoration:

2 tablespoons apricot jam
750 g (1½ lb) marzipan
1 egg white, lightly beaten
1 rounded tablespoon liquid glucose
450 g (1 lb) icing sugar, sifted
cornflour, for sprinkling
red, yellow, and green food colourings

Preparation time: 40 minutes
Cooking time: 3–3½ hours
Oven: 150°C, 300°F, Gas Mark 2

The icing for this cake is simple to make as it is just rolled out and smoothed on. Liquid glucose is available from chemists.

1. Grease and double line a 20 cm (8 inch) cake tin.
2. Place all the cake ingredients into a large mixing bowl. Stir the ingredients to mix them, then beat for about 5 minutes until evenly blended.
3. Place the cake mixture into the prepared cake tin and smooth the top with the back of a metal spoon.
4. Bake in a preheated oven for 3–3½ hours, until the cake is firm to the touch and a skewer inserted into the centre comes out clean. Leave the cake to cool in the tin.
5. Roll out half the marzipan to 2.5 cm (1 inch) larger than the top of the cake. Brush the marzipan with apricot jam and invert the cake on to it. Press the surplus marzipan into the cake with a palette knife, so that the top is flat and the sides are squared off smoothly. Trim off any excess marzipan.
6. Roll out the remaining marzipan to the height and circumference of the cake. Brush the marzipan with jam and place around the side of the cake. Place the cake on a cake board.
7. To make the icing, place the egg white and liquid glucose in a bowl. Add the icing sugar gradually, beating the mixture with a wooden spoon after each addition. As the mixture begins to bind together, knead with the fingers until it forms a smooth ball.
8. Sprinkle a surface with cornflour and knead the icing until it is smooth and pliable.
9. Roll out the icing to 5 cm (2 inches) larger than the top of the cake and place on top of the cake. With cornfloured hands rub in a circular movement over the icing to make it thinner. Work the icing down the sides of the cake to cover it evenly.
10. Trim off the surplus icing with a sharp knife and place in a plastic bag to prevent it from drying out.
11. Colour 3 pieces of the surplus icing yellow, red and green by kneading a few drops of colouring into each piece. Roll out the red piece and cut a candle shape from it. Place in the centre of the cake.
12. Cut some holly leaves from the green icing. Shape berries from the red icing and a candle flame from the yellow icing. Arrange the holly and berries around the base of the candle. Place a small strip of red icing in the centre of the candle flame.
13. Place a ribbon around the cake and tie in a bow. The iced cake will keep for up to 2 weeks, if covered loosely with greaseproof paper.

Christmas candle cake; Farmhouse fruit cake

BLACK CHERRY BEIGNETS

Serves 4–6
450 g (1 lb) black cherries, stoned
100 g (4 oz) sugar
3 tablespoons water
2 tablespoons redcurrant jelly
1 cinnamon stick
150 ml (¼ pint) red wine
1 quantity Choux pastry (opposite)
oil, for deep frying
caster sugar, for sprinkling

Preparation time: 20 minutes
Cooking time: 30–35 minutes

1. Place the cherries in a saucepan with the sugar, water, redcurrant jelly, cinnamon stick and red wine.
2. Heat gently until just boiling, then simmer for 20 minutes. Remove the cinnamon stick and leave the sauce to cool slightly.
3. Heat the oil to 180°C, 350°F, or until a cube of bread rises instantly to the surface. Drop teaspoonsful of choux pastry, a few at a time, into the fat and fry until puffy and golden, about 2 minutes. Drain on kitchen paper and keep warm while frying the remaining beignets.
4. Place the beignets in a serving dish and sprinkle with caster sugar. Place the warm cherry sauce in a jug and serve separately.

CLOCKWISE FROM THE TOP: Black cherry beignets; Choux buns with Chocolate éclairs variation

CHOUX BUNS [M]

Makes 12
Choux pastry:
50 g (2 oz) butter
150 ml (¼ pint) water
65 g (2½ oz) plain flour
2 eggs, beaten
Filling:
1 egg
50 g (2 oz) caster sugar
40 g (1½ oz) plain flour
300 ml (½ pint) milk
25 g (1 oz) butter
few drops of vanilla essence
Decoration:
50 g (2 oz) plain chocolate
icing sugar, for sprinkling

Preparation time: 30 minutes
Cooking time: 30–35 minutes
Oven: 220°C, 425°F, Gas Mark 7;
      190°C, 375°F, Gas Mark 5

1. To make the pastry, place the butter and water in a small saucepan. Heat gently until the butter has melted, then bring to the boil.
2. Tip the flour into the liquid and immediately remove the pan from the heat. Beat quickly with a wooden spoon, until the mixture forms a smooth ball and comes away from the side of the pan.
3. Cool the mixture slightly, then beat in the eggs, a little at a time.
4. Place 12 spoonsful of the mixture, well apart on a greased baking sheet. Bake in a preheated oven for 10 minutes, then reduce the heat and cook for a further 20–25 minutes, until the buns are crisp and golden.
5. Place the buns on a wire tray and pierce the sides with a knife. This will allow the steam to escape and prevent the buns from becoming soggy.
6. To make the filling, place the egg and sugar in a bowl and whisk until frothy. Whisk in the flour and 1 tablespoon of the milk.
7. Heat the remaining milk and pour over the mixture, stirring continuously. Return the mixture to the pan and cook over a moderate heat, stirring until the custard is thickened and smooth.
8. Remove from the heat and beat in the butter and a few drops of vanilla essence. Cover with cling film and leave until cold.
9. When cold fill the buns with the custard through the opening, using a teaspoon.
10. Break up the chocolate and place in a small basin. Set the basin over a pan of hot water and leave until the chocolate has just melted. Spoon the chocolate into a greaseproof paper piping bag and snip off the end.
11. Drizzle the chocolate over the top of each bun. When the chocolate is set, sift a little icing sugar over the top.

Variation:
Chocolate Eclairs: Place the choux pastry in a piping bag fitted with a large plain tube. Pipe about eight 10 cm (4 inch) lengths, well apart, on to a greased baking sheet. Bake as above.
Fill with custard cream or whipped cream.
Melt 100 g (4 oz) chocolate in a bowl over a saucepan of hot water. Dip the top of each eclair into the chocolate to coat.

PARIS BREST

Serves 6–8
1 quantity Choux pastry (left)
25 g (1 oz) flaked almonds
50 g (2 oz) caster sugar
50 g (2 oz) unblanched almonds
300 ml (½ pint) double or whipping cream
icing sugar, for sprinkling

Preparation time: 25 minutes
Cooking time: 45 minutes
Oven: 220°C, 425°F, Gas Mark 7;
      190°C, 375°F, Gas Mark 5

1. Place the choux pastry in a piping bag fitted with a large plain tube. Pipe a 20 cm (8 inch) ring of the pastry on to a greased baking sheet. Pipe a second inside the first one and a third ring on top between the two.
2. Sprinkle the pastry with flaked almonds and bake in a preheated oven for 10 minutes, then reduce the heat and cook for a further 30 minutes, until the ring is well risen, crisp and golden brown.
3. Split the pastry ring in half and place the top beside the base on the baking sheet. Return to the oven at the lower temperature for 5 minutes. Cool on a wire tray.
4. Place the sugar and unblanched almonds in a heavy-based saucepan. Heat gently until the sugar has dissolved and turned golden brown. Pour the mixture on to an oiled baking sheet and leave until cold. Finely crush with a rolling pin or use a liquidiser.
5. Whip the cream until stiff, then fold in the praline. Place the base of the pastry ring on a serving plate and fill with the cream mixture. Cover with the top of the ring.
6. Dust the pastry ring with sifted icing sugar and chill until ready to serve. It is best eaten the day it is made.

GINGER MARMALADE CAKE

Serves 10–12
200 ml (⅓ pint) vegetable oil
175 g (6 oz) ginger marmalade
175 g (6 oz) caster sugar
3 eggs, beaten
4 tablespoons milk
175 g (6 oz) wholewheat flour
175 g (6 oz) self-raising flour
1 teaspoon baking powder
50 g (2 oz) crystallized ginger, chopped, for topping

Preparation time: 10 minutes
Cooking time: 1½–1¾ hours
Oven: 160°C, 325°F, Gas Mark 3

1. Grease and line a 20 cm (8 inch) round cake tin.
2. Place all the cake ingredients in a mixing bowl. Beat for about 2 minutes until well mixed.
3. Place into the prepared tin and smooth the top. Sprinkle evenly with the crystallized ginger.
4. Bake in a preheated oven for 1½–1¾ hours, until the cake is golden brown and firm to the touch.
5. Cool in the tin for 15 minutes, then cool completely on a wire tray.

FROSTED ORANGE SQUARES

Makes 20
225 g (8 oz) butter, melted or 250 ml (8 fl oz) vegetable oil
300 ml (½ pint) unsweetened orange juice
275 g (10 oz) caster sugar
2 eggs, beaten
400 g (14 oz) self-raising flour
Topping:
100 g (4 oz) icing sugar
3 tablespoons unsweetened orange juice

Preparation time: 10 minutes
Cooking time: 1 hour
Oven: 180°C, 350°F, Gas Mark 4

1. Grease and bottom-line a 20 cm × 25 cm (8 inches × 10 inches) roasting tin.
2. Place all the cake ingredients in a bowl. Beat well until smooth and evenly mixed.
3. Pour into the tin and bake in a preheated oven for 1 hour, until firm and golden brown.
4. To make the topping, place the icing sugar and orange juice in a bowl and beat together until smooth. Pour the topping over the warm cake and leave in the tin to cool completely.
5. When cold, cut into 5 cm (2 inch) squares.

ROUND BATTENBURG CAKE

Serves 8–10
175 g (6 oz) self-raising flour
1 teaspoon baking powder
175 g (6 oz) caster sugar
175 g (6 oz) soft margarine
3 eggs
few drops of red food colouring
Filling and decoration:
4 tablespoons apricot jam
350 g (12 oz) marzipan
marzipan fruits, to decorate

Preparation time: 25 minutes
Cooking time: 30–35 minutes
Oven: 180°C, 350°F, Gas Mark 4

1. Grease and bottom-line two 20 cm (8 inch) sandwich tins.
2. Place the flour, baking powder, sugar, margarine and eggs in a bowl. Beat with a wooden spoon until light and fluffy, about 3 minutes (or 1 minute with a mixer). Place half the mixture in one of the prepared tins.
3. Colour the remaining mixture pink with a few drops of red food colouring. Place in the other tin. Smooth the tops of the cakes and bake in a preheated oven for 30–35 minutes, until golden brown and firm to the touch.
4. Leave the cakes in the tins for 1 minute, then turn out on to a wire tray to cool completely.
5. Using a large cup as a guide, cut out a 10 cm (4 inch) circle from the centre of each cake.
6. Spread a little apricot jam around the side of each circle. Place the pink circle in the plain cake and vice versa.
7. Sandwich the cakes together with apricot jam. Spread the remaining jam over the top and sides of the cake.
8. Roll out half the marzipan to cover the top of the cake. Use the remaining marzipan to cover the sides. Pinch the join at the top edge of cake between finger and thumb to form a decorative border.
9. Place some marzipan fruits around the top edge of the cake, sticking with a little jam if necessary.

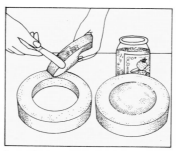 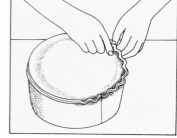

Spreading centre with jam   Fluting the marzipan covering

Round Battenburg cake; Frosted orange squares

GINGER WHIRLS

Makes 40

275 g (10 oz) self-raising flour
3 teaspoons ground ginger
1 teaspoon bicarbonate of soda
75 g (3 oz) caster sugar
3 tablespoons golden syrup
2 tablespoons black treacle
75 g (3 oz) butter or margarine, melted
1 egg, beaten
25 g (1 oz) demerara sugar

Preparation time: 15 minutes, plus chilling
Cooking time: 10–12 minutes
Oven: 180°C, 350°F, Gas Mark 4

Once this biscuit mixture is rolled up it can be wrapped in greaseproof paper and foil and stored in the refrigerator for 2 weeks or frozen for 3 months.

1. Sift the flour, ginger and bicarbonate of soda into a bowl. Stir in the caster sugar. Add the syrup, treacle, melted butter or margarine and beaten egg and mix to a soft dough.
2. Knead the dough lightly on a floured surface. Place the dough on a large piece of floured foil or non-stick silicone paper and roll out to form an oblong 30 cm × 39 cm (12 inches × 15 inches).
3. Sprinkle the dough evenly with the demerara sugar. Using the foil or paper to help you, roll up the dough from one long edge. Wrap the dough in the foil or paper and chill for 2 hours.
4. Using a sharp knife, thinly slice off rounds of dough and place a little apart, on a greased baking sheet.
5. Bake in a preheated oven for 10–12 minutes, until slightly risen. Leave the biscuits on the baking sheets for 5 minutes, then lift with a palette knife and transfer to a wire tray to cool. Once cold, store the biscuits in an airtight tin.

APPLE AND ORANGE FLAN

Serves 4–6
175 g (6 oz) plain flour
25 g (1 oz) caster sugar
75 g (3 oz) softened butter or soft margarine
1 egg, beaten
Filling:
1 orange
450 g (1 lb) firm eating apples (e.g. Cox's, Golden Delicious)
150 ml (¼ pint) single cream
2 eggs
50 g (2 oz) caster sugar

Preparation time: 20 minutes, plus chilling
Cooking time: 40 minutes
Oven: 220°C, 425°F, Gas Mark 7;
  200°C, 400°F, Gas Mark 6

1. Place the flour, sugar, butter or margarine and beaten egg in a bowl. Mix with a fork to form a soft dough.
2. Knead the dough lightly on a floured surface, then wrap in cling film and chill for 1 hour.
3. Roll out and line a 23 cm (9 inch) flan tin.
4. To make the filling, finely grate the orange rind and squeeze the juice. Peel, quarter and core the apples, then cut into slices and toss in the orange juice.
5. Arrange the apples in overlapping circles around the base of the flan case. Bake in a preheated oven for 10 minutes.
6. Place the orange rind, cream, eggs and sugar in a bowl and beat together. Pour the mixture into the flan case.
7. Reduce the oven temperature and cook the flan for a further 30 minutes, until the pastry is golden brown and the filling has set. Serve warm or cold.

CHERRY STRUDEL

Serves 12
300 g (11 oz) plain flour
½ teaspoon salt
1 egg, beaten
1 tablespoon oil
150 ml (¼ pint) warm water
Filling:
1 kg (2 lb) cherries, stoned
50 g (2 oz) flaked almonds
225 g (8 oz) raisins
100 g (4 oz) caster sugar
1 teaspoon ground cinnamon
50 g (2 oz) butter, melted
icing sugar, for sprinkling

Preparation time: 25 minutes, plus resting
Cooking time: 40 minutes
Oven: 200°C, 400°F, Gas Mark 6

1. Place the flour and salt in a bowl. Make a well in the centre and add the beaten egg, oil and water. Beat the ingredients together to form a soft dough.
2. Place the dough in an oiled polythene bag and rest at room temperature for 1 hour.
3. To make the filling, place all the ingredients in a bowl and mix together.
4. Roll out one half of the dough on a floured surface to form a 20 cm (8 inch) square. Carefully stretch the dough with the hands until it is almost transparent and measures 45 cm × 30 cm (18 inches × 12 inches). Cut off any thick edges.
5. Brush the dough with melted butter and spread on half the filling. Roll up from one long edge and lift carefully on to a greased baking sheet. Repeat with the remaining dough and filling.
6. Brush with melted butter and bake in a preheated oven for 40 minutes, until light golden and crisp.
7. Cool on the baking sheet for 10 minutes, then transfer to a wire tray to cool completely. Sprinkle with icing sugar and cut each strudel into 6 pieces.

CRUNCHY CHEESECAKE TART

Serves 6
50 g (2 oz) butter or margarine, melted
100 g (4 oz) shortcake biscuits, crushed
15 g (½ oz) chopped walnuts
Filling and decoration:
225 g (8 oz) full fat soft cheese, softened
50 g (2 oz) caster sugar
2 eggs, beaten
grated rind and juice of 1 lemon
225 g (8 oz) fresh fruit, e.g. strawberries, grapes, satsumas, sliced bananas, kiwi fruit

Preparation time: 20 minutes
Cooking time: 30–35 minutes
Oven: 190°C, 375°F, Gas Mark 5

1. In a bowl, mix together the melted butter or margarine, biscuit crumbs and chopped walnuts. Press the mixture over the base and sides of a 20 cm (8 inch) ovenproof pie plate or flan dish.
2. To make the filling, place the cheese, sugar, beaten eggs, lemon rind and juice in a bowl. Whisk until smooth, preferably with an electric whisk.
3. Pour the mixture into the biscuit base and bake in a preheated oven for 30–35 minutes, until the filling has just set. Leave to cool.
4. Decorate the top of the cheesecake with circles of a selection of fresh fruit.

Crunchy cheesecake tart; Apple and orange flan; Cherry strudel

BROWN SODA BREAD

Makes 1 large or 2 small loaves
450 g (1 lb) wholewheat flour
225 g (8 oz) plain flour
1 teaspoon bicarbonate of soda
1 teaspoon salt
600 ml (1 pint) buttermilk

Preparation time: 5 minutes
Cooking time: 35–45 minutes
Oven: 200°C, 400°F, Gas Mark 6

1. Sift both the flours and the bicarbonate of soda into a bowl. Add the salt and rub the ingredients between the hands to mix thoroughly.
2. Add the buttermilk, all at once, and mix lightly to form a soft dough.
3. Knead briefly, then shape into 1 large or 2 small rounds. Cut a deep cross in the top of the bread.
4. Dust the bread with flour and place on a floured baking sheet.
5. Bake in a preheated oven for 35 minutes for the small loaves or 45 minutes for the large one, until the bread is well browned and sounds hollow when tapped on the base.
6. Cool on a wire tray. Eat the day it is made if possible.

DROP SCONES

Makes about 25
225 g (8 oz) self-raising flour
2 teaspoons baking powder
pinch of salt
25 g (1 oz) caster sugar
1 egg
300 ml (½ pint) milk

Preparation time: 5 minutes
Cooking time: about 4 minutes

1. Sift the flour, baking powder and salt into a bowl. Stir in the sugar.
2. Make a well in the centre of the flour and drop in the egg. Gradually beat in the milk to form a fairly thick batter.
3. Lightly grease a griddle or heavy-based frying pan. Place over a moderate heat.
4. Drop tablespoonsful of the batter on to the pan, a little distance apart and cook until bubbles appear on the surface of the scones. Turn and cook on the other side for about 1 minute.
5. Keep the scones warm while cooking the remaining batter. Serve warm, with butter and preserves.

QUICK SCONES

Makes 10
225 g (8 oz) self-raising flour
1 teaspoon baking powder
50 g (2 oz) soft margarine
25 g (1 oz) caster sugar
150 ml (¼ pint) milk
milk, to glaze

Preparation time: 10 minutes
Cooking time: 12–15 minutes
Oven: 220°C, 425°F, Gas Mark 7

Using soft margarine enables all the ingredients for the dough to be added together, so that the scones are quickly prepared.

1. Sift the flour and baking powder into a bowl. Add the margarine, sugar and milk and mix to a soft dough.
2. Place on a floured surface and knead lightly. Roll out to a 1 cm (½ inch) thickness and cut into rounds with a 6 cm (2½ inch) fluted pastry cutter.
3. Place the scones on a greased baking sheet and bake in a preheated oven for 12–15 minutes, until well risen and golden brown. Serve warm, split and buttered.

Drop scones; Walnut brownies; American bran muffins

WALNUT BROWNIES

Makes 16 squares
50 g (2 oz) plain chocolate
75 g (3 oz) butter
225 g (8 oz) caster sugar
2 eggs, beaten
1 teaspoon vanilla essence
75 g (3 oz) plain flour
½ teaspoon baking powder
½ teaspoon salt
50 g (2 oz) walnuts, chopped

Preparation time: 15 minutes
Cooking time: 35 minutes
Oven: 190°C, 375°F, Gas Mark 5

1. Grease and bottom-line a 20 cm (8 inch) square tin.
2. Break up the chocolate and place in a mixing bowl with the butter and sugar. Place the bowl over a pan of hot water until the chocolate has melted.
3. Add the remaining ingredients and beat until smooth. Pour the mixture into the prepared tin.
4. Bake in a preheated oven for 35 minutes, until firm around the edges. Cool in the tin, then cut into squares. Eat the same day if possible.

AMERICAN BRAN MUFFINS

Makes 20
4 tablespoons oil
75 g (3 oz) soft dark brown sugar
75 g (3 oz) golden syrup
2 eggs, beaten
250 ml (8 fl oz) milk
50 g (2 oz) bran
75 g (3 oz) raisins
100 g (4 oz) self-raising flour
1 teaspoon baking powder
½ teaspoon bicarbonate of soda
½ teaspoon salt

Preparation time: 10 minutes
Cooking time: 15 minutes
Oven: 200°C, 400°F, Gas Mark 6

1. Place the oil, sugar, syrup, beaten eggs and milk in a large bowl. Mix thoroughly with a fork.
2. Add the bran and raisins and sift in the flour, baking powder, bicarbonate of soda and salt. Stir very lightly until the ingredients are just mixed.
3. Spoon the mixture into paper cake cases or greased muffin tins until two-thirds full.
4. Bake in a preheated oven for 15 minutes, until well risen and firm to the touch. Serve warm, split in half and buttered.

INDEX